Susan Anna Wheeler

Daughters of Armenia

Susan Anna Wheeler

Daughters of Armenia

ISBN/EAN: 9783337292829

Printed in Europe, USA, Canada, Australia, Japan

Cover: Foto ©Lupo / pixelio.de

More available books at **www.hansebooks.com**

Daughters of Armenia.

By Mrs. S. A. Wheeler,
MISSIONARY IN TURKEY.

"On the banks of the ancient Euphrates,
 Where woman fell under God's frown,
Armenia's Daughters are coming,
 Their King and Redeemer to crown."

American Tract Society,
150 NASSAU STREET, NEW YORK.

COPYRIGHT, 1877,
BY AMERICAN TRACT SOCIETY.

INTRODUCTION.

At a time when so much is said concerning woman's place and work in the church, and when especially our sisters, young and old, are waking up to new interest in foreign missions, a little volume of facts and incidents, showing what may be, by what has been accomplished in one part of the wide world-field, we believe can not fail to be acceptable and useful. While making those who already feel an interest in this work, more intelligent in regard to its methods and successes, and thus more efficient in planning, laboring and praying for it, we hope to do much to convince those hitherto indifferent, of their responsibility, and also to encourage the little ones to do their part in the holy and blessed work of bringing back a lost world to Jesus.

How many unhappy, because practically useless lives are there even among Christian women, who if once possessed by an intelligent enthusiasm to labor for Christ, abroad or at home, would, while doing good service for the Master, bless their own souls with a fulness of joy hitherto unknown.

To aid in giving such joy to her Christian sisters in America, and to their children, the author affectionately dedicates this little volume to them, praying that her labor of love may not be in vain in the Lord.

A MISSIONARY.

CONTENTS.

CHAPTER I.
Who are the Armenians? - - - - - - - - - - - - - - - - - - PAGE 7

CHAPTER II.
Religion of the Armenians - 14

CHAPTER III.
How we Reached the Women - - - - - - - - - - - - - - - - - 28

CHAPTER IV.
The Best Way to Help Them - - - - - - - - - - - - - - - - - - 38

CHAPTER V.
The Village-School Teacher - - - - - - - - - - - - - - - - - - 48

CHAPTER VI.
Mariam, the Hoghi Bible-Woman - - - - - - - - - - - - - - 60

CHAPTER VII.
Visit to Hoghi - 72

CHAPTER VIII.
Light in Dark Homes - 81

CONTENTS.

CHAPTER IX.
A Visit to Ichmeh ---------------------------------- 93

CHAPTER X.
Across the Euphrates ------------------------------- 101

CHAPTER XI.
At the Feast --------------------------------------- 109

CHAPTER XII.
Gulaser's Household -------------------------------- 116

CHAPTER XIII.
Tour Continued and Ended --------------------------- 128

CHAPTER XIV.
Does it Pay? --------------------------------------- 142

DAUGHTERS OF ARMENIA.

CHAPTER I.

WHO ARE THE ARMENIANS?

THIS question my little girl asked me one day as we were sitting together at our work; and perhaps my little readers will like to know what I said to her.

Susie was born in Armenia, for her papa and mamma were missionaries in that country; but when she came to America on a visit, the people would insist on calling her "a little Turk." She remembered the people who came to her papa's meetings and to mamma's school, and she knew they were not Turks; and yet she could not explain the difference; so she did as most children do, and as it is very proper they should so, she came and asked mother.

"Besides," she said, "the folks say the Turks

are very cruel and wicked. Are they, mamma? We used to go to their vineyards, and they were very kind to us. They gave us fruits and sweet drink, and brought cushions for us to sit upon under the trees. Did you not think Hassan Agha and his wife very pleasant people? And you know, mamma, that Mahmet, their boy, made brother Willie a good many curious little toys. He always seemed so pleasant when he came to our house that I never felt afraid of him, and yet I know he was a Turk.

"And the Turks are not black and ugly-looking, as some here seem to think, are they, mamma? I wish they could see the pretty girl who used to bring us sour milk when we were at our summer-room; you know, the one who married a captain in the Turkish army. How beautiful she looked when she called upon us one day in the city with her mother. You had some cake and tea brought, and she threw her long veil back, and we could see her bright orange silk jacket and the jewels on her neck and wrists, and her eyes so black and soft. She was not ugly-looking, I am sure.

"Mamma, what makes the people hate the Turks? Papa read in the newspaper the other day about a minister in England, who said, 'It is time the Turks were wiped out of the earth.' It must be he did not know much about them. Perhaps he had only heard about the wicked soldiers who killed the poor Bulgarians, and felt angry with all the Turks. Don't you think it would have been better if he had prayed that they might all become Christians, and learn war no more?"

Susie chatted on awhile, bringing up pleasant memories of our home in the East; and then recollecting she had begun with an important question, she waited for the answer.

I think myself the Turks are a very interesting people, and hope the time is not far distant when they will become Christians. Now they are Mohammedans, or followers of Mohammed. They believe in God, but not in Jesus Christ. They acknowledge that Christ was a prophet, but not so great as Mohammed, and they will not receive Him as the Son of God. But we will not talk about them to-day. As we began about the Armenians, I will explain to you who they are.

If you will get the Bible and turn to the third verse of the tenth chapter of Genesis, you will find the name Togarmah mentioned as a grandson of Japheth, one of the sons of Noah. Perhaps Togarmah used to sit on his grandfather's knee and listen while he told him about the ark that his father built; how the people laughed at him, and even the carpenters mockingly asked where he would find water enough to float such a large, awkward ship. And how interested he must have been to hear about the animals coming, two and two, to enter the ark, and how the very heavens were black with the birds that came flying in from every quarter. Then when everything was ready, how Noah was directed to take all his family in, and that God himself shut the door, so that it could not be opened till the flood was passed. Perhaps he asked, with wistful look and a tearful eye, about those that were left out, and his grandfather told him with sad tones how they begged to be taken in, but the door was shut, so that Noah could not open it, though he was very sorry for them.

After he had listened to these stories, how beautiful the rainbow must have looked to Togarmah as it spanned the heavens with its bright belt after a heavy rain, which perhaps made him think God would again drown the world; and how he thanked God, who had set his sign in the clouds to assure us that he would no more destroy the earth with a flood. The rainbow, I have no doubt, seemed more to him than it does to us, and brighter too, for it looks much brighter in Turkey than in this part of the world. It is because the atmosphere is clearer. The heavens at night, when the moon is absent, are very brilliant, and I have seen sunsets there when it seemed as if the very "gates of glory" were opened in the western sky.

Before we shut up the Bible let us turn to the twenty-fourth verse of the same chapter, and there let me introduce to you one of Togarmah's cousins, young Eber, or Heber. He is about the same age as Togarmah, but his face has a little more of the olive hue, though they resemble each other. Eber's father was a son of Shem, the brother of Japheth. These boys, I dare say, played together often at the foot of Mount Ararat, where the ark rested after the flood. Perhaps they sometimes climbed up the steep sides to find some relic of the old home of their grandfather.

The people of those days must often have talked about the deluge, and believed it had been, for we find by the Bible that some of them very soon planned to build a tower that would reach up to heaven, so that if another flood should come they might all be safe. Then God was displeased; for had he not promised that this should never be, putting his own seal on his promise, the beautiful rain bow of which I have just spoken? He sent a confusion of tongues among these unbelieving builders, and they were scattered in the earth. Eber went towards the northwest, and settled in Ur of the Chaldees, and Abraham, the father of the Hebrew or Jewish nation, came from him. Togarmah went towards the north, and we read about his descendants in Ezekiel, with other great nations, as bringing merchandise to the great, proud city of Tyre. History tells us that the people who descended from Togarmah became a brave and warlike nation, ruling over a large part of Asia Minor. The last king of this people died more than a hundred years before America was discovered by Columbus, and since then they have been a subjected nation, often suffering from hard and hopeless oppression.

And now perhaps you will ask, as Susie did, how we found out all this. I will tell you. Partly from the Bible, partly from books of history, and also from writings and images carved on rocks and on the ruins of forts, castles, and bridges all through that country. These are very curious and abundant.

But in spite of changes and sufferings, this people retain much of their nobleness of character and their love of religion. They have lost, in some re-

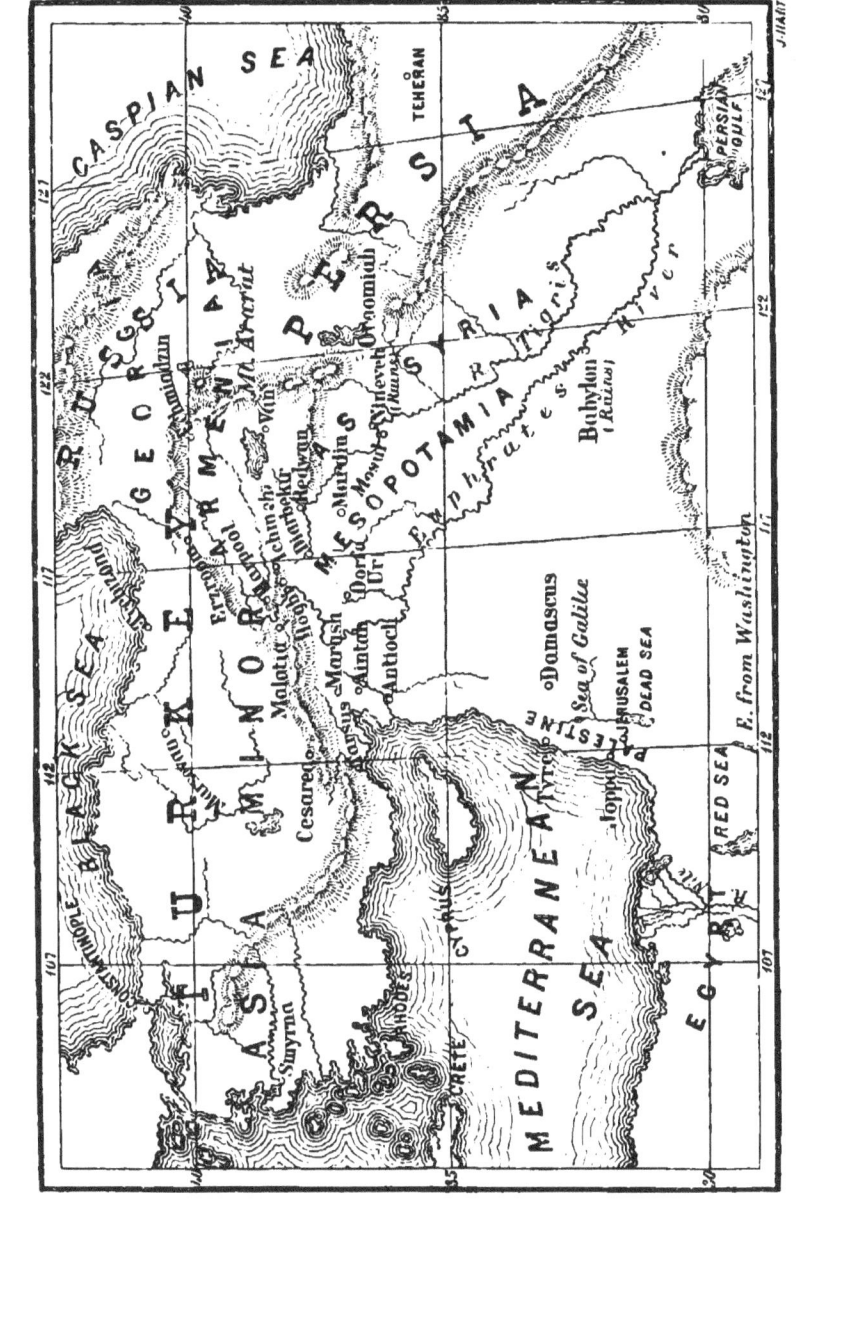

gions, their national language, but have preserved their customs and habits. They are industrious, perhaps more so than any other nation in Asia Minor. Dr. Dwight calls them the Anglo-Saxons of that land, and thinks them among the most hopeful of the many nations found in the Turkish empire. They are very patriotic. Their national hymns often bring tears to the eyes of strangers.

Now I have told you who these Armenians are; if you will take your map, we will see if we can find their country. There it is, bounded on the north by the Black sea and Georgia, a province in Russia; on the east by the Caspian sea; on the south by Mesopotamia and Assyria; and on the west by Asia Minor. Their country has been conquered and divided between three governments, Persia, Russia, and Turkey, the territories of the three joining at Mount Ararat, which you see on the map.

CHAPTER II.

THE RELIGION OF THE ARMENIANS.

"MAMMA, what was the earliest religion of the Armenians?" said Susie to me one day. "Were they Mohammedans, like the Turks?"

No, indeed! Mohammedanism did not arise till the seventh century, while the Armenians became Christians hundreds of years before. Their earliest religion was idolatry. And so was that of the Turks, a conquering horde from Tartary, who about the tenth century overran Armenia, and afterwards Asia Minor. These Turks early adopted the faith of Mohammed, but the Armenians did not. They look upon those who turn from Christianity to Mohammedanism as most infamous in character, and beyond all hope of salvation through Christ. I have heard them say that to become a Mohammedan is to commit the unpardonable sin spoken of in the Bible.

But to understand better about the Armenians we must go back to the first century. They had forgotten the God of Noah and of Japheth, and had turned from the worship of the Creator to created things. If we go to the banks of the old Hiddekel, or Tigris, we find a large Armenian graveyard, where the peculiar form of the gravestones shows that the people buried there were once sun-worshippers. Their own history says that they have been converted to Christianity twice. The first time was during the life of our Saviour upon earth. One of their kings, Abgar by name, heard of the miracles of Christ, believed on him, and sent to this "wonderful man" to come and visit him, promising, if he would come, to give him rest and protection from all his enemies. If you will turn to John 12:20, 21, you will read of some men called Greeks, who came to Philip, and said, "Sir, we would see Jesus." It is affirmed that these were King Abgar's messengers. They were called Greeks, because they resembled them and spoke their language; just the same as they are now called Turks by some persons, because they speak the Turkish language. At the Centennial last summer we heard a good deal said of the Turks who were present; and they were not Turks at all, but Greeks and Armenians. The evangelists wrote just as we should under similar circumstances.

Their history goes on to say that Thaddeus,

one of the apostles, went to Edessa, their chief city, and preached the gospel, and that the people became Christians at that time.

But they must have gone back from following Christ, for we find that three hundred years later the Christian bishop Gregory found them idolaters, and was the means of restoring them to Christianity. Susie remembers hearing about Gregory the Illuminator. The Armenians call St. Gregory their patron saint. He was a member of the royal family, and secretary of King Tiridates. When he became a Christian, the king was very angry with him, and because he refused longer to take part in idolatrous worship, he commanded him to be imprisoned in a gloomy cave, where he was kept for fourteen years. The king, being afterwards greatly afflicted with a severe malady, his conscience upbraided him for his cruelty to his secretary and friend Gregory, and he sent to the cave and released him. It is said the king was healed of his disease and became a Christian, and commanded all his court to embrace this religion and to be baptized in the name of Christ. This was about the year 318, and since that time the Armenians have been a Christian nation.

They did not have the Bible in their own language for two hundred years after that, when a learned monk, by the name of Mesrob, invented an alphabet, and translated the Bible for them. I do not know if they had any books before that time, but we still find inscriptions on rocks and on the walls of the old city Diarbekir which are written in the old Armenian language.

Mesrob lived in Palu, a small city on the Euphrates, about forty miles east of Harpoot. This city is built around the base of a mountain which rises up in the midst of it like a great sugar-loaf. In the face of a lofty cliff at the top of this sugar loaf is a cave, in which the learned and pious Mesrob translated the Bible from the Syriac and Greek languages. It was probably one of the first books written with the new alphabet. It was completed about the year 431, but was not printed till more than twelve hundred years after, when in 1666 Bishop Uscan was sent to Amsterdam to take charge of the printing.

All this time they used it in the manuscript form, and we still find copies most beautifully written on very nice parchment, plainer and more easily read than the printed copies. There is one very old Bible we used to find wrapped up in several embroidered napkins, and put carefully into a box behind the altar, in one of the old churches. But I do not know its history.

They did not put their manuscripts into rolls, as the Jews did, but bound them into books like ours, and they were often illustrated by pictures made with the pen in blue, red, and green ink. And at this time they made many other books. Historians tell us that this fifth century was the golden age of Armenian literature. The Bible had the same influence on their literature as the Wickliffe Bible—the first English translation—had on our own.

Dr. Riggs of Constantinople gave them the Bible they now have, translated into the modern or spoken tongue. This was a much needed work, for many of the people could not understand the language as it was spoken by the learned or by the bishops and teachers. Many of the priests were very ignorant, and could not read intelligently the Bible found in their churches. You may wonder at this; but books were few comparatively, and costly, and they had no schools for all classes as we have. The people were therefore very ignorant, and did n't care much if their priest was ignorant too.

They did not use the Bible much in their

churches, but read more from a book of ceremonies. Doubtless there were many things in this book grounded upon the Bible; and even when Gregory preached the gospel to them it was mixed with much that is taught in the Romish church, and which we do not receive because it is not taught in the word of God. For instance, they pray to the virgin Mary and the other saints. They think these are near to Christ, and he will surely hear them. Some of the poor women have often said to me, "What should we do without the Virgin? She was a woman like us, and knows how to pity us when we are in sorrow."

They also pray for the dead; for, though they do not believe in what the Romanists call purgatory, they seem to think that in some way, if the priests go and pray near the grave, it will be better for their friends.

In their church they are taught, too, that baptism is regeneration, and that they cannot enter heaven if unbaptized. Doubtless Gregory meant to teach that the outward seal was the acknowledgment of the inward work of the Holy Spirit; but if he did, they have now become content with the mere outward form.

The great head of their church, called the Catholicos, lives in Russia, and all the bishops have to go to him for ordination ; then they are qualified to ordain the priests. There are two orders of priests. The higher order, called vartabeds, and the bishops, are not allowed to marry, but live in monasteries, or in rooms connected with the church. But the ordinary priest is not ordained until he is married, and then he is expected to live among the people, visiting them at their houses and mingling freely among them.

His wife also has a position as priestess. The evening after the priest is ordained the women of the parish come to her house to initiate her into her new position of honor. They have a curious way of doing this.

Twelve cushions are put in the most honorable room in the parsonage, and she is placed upon them and becomes the queen of the evening. These cushions indicate that she is twelve steps higher than any other woman in the parish. She is therefore expected to be leader in all good things which women in that land are expected to know. If the priestess dies, the priest cannot take a second wife, but, if he wishes, he can live in a convent, and become a vartabed or a bishop.

I dare say my young friends would like to know

something of their form of worship. Susie has seen it, and thinks it very queer. If you were to go into one of their churches, you would see one priest walking about among the people, swinging a censer in his hand, burning incense. Another would be intoning prayers, or chanting. Sometimes the priests and bishops are dressed in gaudy robes; and so are the little boys, a number of whom take part in the service. These all make the sign of the cross, burn incense before pictures, and ring little bells. The people keep coming in and going out. The men occupy the lower part of the house. As soon as they reach their places, they make the sign of the cross, fall on their knees, and touch the floor with their foreheads. This they do several times before they give attention to what the priests are doing. The women, in the gallery, behind a lattice, do the same; but they do not give much attention to what the priests say, for it is in the ancient language, which they do not understand. I have been told that they spend much of their time in church in gossiping, or making matches for their marriageable boys and girls.

They have a great many fast-days, and if we should judge them by these, we should think them very good, if, as they suppose, these fasts really make them better. There are one hundred and sixty-five days in the year when they take no meat; this is what they call fasting. Some of these days they keep with far greater care than they do the Sabbath. They have a great many feast-days too.

The observance of all these ceremonies is their way of going to heaven. When they do wrong they go to the priest and confess; and then, if they keep strictly all the forms of the church, they consider themselves safe. And when they are dying, if the priest comes, and dips a piece of consecrated bread in wine, and puts it on their lips, they think they are ready for heaven. How deluded and ignorant are these poor creatures!

And yet, as I have sometimes said, I think there are some real Christians among them.

"Yeghesa's mother," suggests Susie, "how very earnestly she would listen to all you told her about the Lord Jesus."

Yes, I think she was one who really loved the Lord Jesus, though she was very ignorant. She never could seem to give up her hold on the Virgin Mary, though she came to put her in the second place, rather than the first, as she had always done before we tried to teach her. When she was dying she called in the priest to come and give her the communion. She had lived so long in her old faith, that it was hard to give it up; or perhaps it would be better to say, that she could not give up the outward forms, which had become a second nature.

Now all this talk about the religion of this people puzzled Susie. When she heard me say they were Christians, and heard her papa remark that they were a very religious people, she could not understand it.

"It seems to me," said she, "they were real idolaters, and I do n't wonder the Turks call them so, when they see them kissing the cross, burning incense to pictures, and bringing out the bones of the saints on great saints' days, and all that sort of thing. It seems to me they worshipped these and the Virgin Mary, as much as they did Christ. Once I went with Anna to their church, and they had an image of Christ dressed and laid in the grave, and they said he would rise from the dead at Easter. Then they threw a great silver cross into a large trough of water, and Anna said the man who would give the most money, and take it out, would gain a great deal of merit, and be thought very pious. We do 'nt find any such things in the Bible, and I do n't see how papa can call them very religious."

The word *religion* means a system of faith or belief; and any one who adheres very strictly to his system may be said to be very religious. To be religious and to be Christian are two very different things. Paul on Mars' Hill calls the pagan Greeks "very religious," but he did not mean to say they believed in the Bible. One day an Armenian woman in high position came to me, and asked if it was wrong for her to wear her gold. She hoped that she loved Christ, and was soon to be admitted to the Protestant church in Harpoot. I said, "Eughaper, neither taking off nor putting on gold is Christianity. To be a Christian is to be like Christ. If your gold hinders you in this, take it off. If you think it a hindrance to some poor weak sister, I think you would be happier to lay it aside." You see people may be very religious who do not really live as the Bible directs.

The Armenians do believe the Bible. They accept it as God's Book. The name they give to it is *God-breath*, which seems to me very beautiful. I think the masses of the people suppose they are living as the Bible teaches, but they are very ignorant. They know nothing about the new birth. They feel that they are constantly doing as they ought not to, and so are ever anxious to go through all the forms prescribed by their priests and bishops, that, if possible, they may be made better, and fitted for heaven. They think the priests tell them what is in the Bible. The women are more ignorant than the men; so they are more under the influence of the priests, and more careful to do all he bids them, or as I might say, are more religious than the men.

There was one old woman who lived near us, whom we used to see every morning coming from the old church. She was bent almost double, and it seemed hard for her to get along. She was one of the "very religious." I never saw her but I felt rebuked for my own lack of earnestness in the religion of the Bible. I professed to love Christ and to imitate him. I had the Bible, and could read it for myself, yet her zeal seemed far greater than mine. I used to pray that God would show her the right way, and save her in heaven.

There was another very religious woman, I once met with in one of the villages on Harpoot plain. She said, "Lady, I love you, and think you are a real Christian, but one thing you say I cannot receive. You say the virgin Mary is not our intercessor. What should we women do, if we could not call upon the virgin when in trouble, or suffering? She was a woman, and knows how to pity women like us." This is what they all say.

I told her that Jesus, the son of Mary, was also the Son of God, and could do more for us than Mary could; that Mary herself must find salvation through this same Saviour, for "there is no other name given under heaven and among men whereby we can be saved." She was very much shocked that I should think the virgin Mary needed salvation at all. It seemed to her like blasphemy, and I presume she made the sign of the cross many times while talking with me, lest she should be led away by such dreadful heresy.

I do not know if she ever became a Protestant, though at this time her eldest son was a member of the Protestant church, and before she died all her family became Protestants. I think she did change some in her views of Christ as her only Saviour. She loved her eldest son very dearly, and thought he was a better man after he became a Protestant; but the religion of her childhood clung to her to the very last. Her sons had no doubt of her acceptance before God; they felt that she lived very near to the standard which Christ laid down for his disciples.

It seemed to me when I went to Armenia, and

became acquainted with the people and their religion, that they only needed to have the Bible brought to them in a language they could understand, and to be taught to read it, to become as much a Christian nation as our own. They are to me a very interesting people, though when I first reached them all was "strange and new," and at times I felt a little lonely and homesick. When I looked from my window, down the city of Harpoot, with its houses made of sundried bricks, the scene was unlike anything I had ever beheld before. I had read of old ruins and castles, and now I was in the midst of them. The house we lived in seemed more like a great castle than a house. Then the people in the streets, and all around us, and the sounds that greeted my ears made me feel that I was a stranger in a strange land. It did not seemed much like the garden of Eden, that God made so beautiful for Adam and Eve to live in.

"Why, mamma," exclaims Susie, "was that the very same old garden of Eden we read about in Genesis?"

"To be sure. Read Genesis 2:10–14, and you will see why so many people believe that it was just there."

CHAPTER III.

HOW WE REACHED THE WOMEN.

It seemed strange to Susie, and I dare say will appear quite as strange to you, my young readers, to learn that though the Armenians have the Bible, they are very ignorant of its contents; and this is particularly true of the women. When I went to my missionary work in Harpoot twenty years ago, I did not find a single woman who could read the Bible. They did not think it was written for women at all.

One woman went to her priest or minister, and asked him if it was wrong for her to learn to read it. She had heard that the women in some parts of their land had begun to do so, and she desired very much to read it herself. Her priest replied, "Are you going to be a priest that you should read the Bible?" She made no answer to him, but hastened away lest he should question her and find out the longing in her heart, and forbid her.

Missionaries had been laboring among this people many years before we went there, and the women in many parts of the country were acquiring a knowledge of the blessed Book. But in Harpoot, where we were sent, the work was new.

It was quite hard to get at the women at first. They did not come to see us; they were afraid of us. They said we were wicked women. "Do you not know that these women that read are leather-faces? See their uncovered, shameless faces. Do you wish to be like them?" their priests would say, to keep them from coming to us. And when we went into the streets they would call to one another, "The women who wear washbowls on their heads are coming." Then the boys would gather at the corners, and sometimes a stone would go whistling by us, and they would run and cry out, "Prote! Prote!" (Protestant.) Sometimes a stream of dirty water would come down from a high roof, and we would just escape an unpleasant showerbath. Perhaps they would exclaim, "Beg your pardon, we did not see you," but we knew it was meant as an insult.

One day I went out with a woman who had become a Protestant, and as we were passing through a ward of the city where I was a stranger, several children stopped, looked at me for a moment, and then cried out, "Shatan," (Satan,) "Jeen! Jeen!" and ran away as fast as they could. I asked the woman what they meant by "Jeen." "The evil one," she replied: "did you not see how they ran? They were afraid of you."

Perhaps some of you may think these things would make me laugh, or else make me angry. But no, I pitied them. I did not feel much like "the evil one," for I had gone out to call on their mothers and try to persuade them to read the Bible, and to let their children come to the schools we wished to help them open. I knew that all this fear and ignorance was because they did not know God's blessed word.

By-and-by, however, after a long time, they overcame their fears and prejudice enough to come to our home. They wanted to see how we lived, how we dressed, and what we ate. They would sometimes pull at our braided hair, and say, "Why do you put up your hair in a knot at the back of your head? We wear ours in small braids down our backs." We told them custom made us to differ. Then they would examine my dress so closely, that I had to say to them very decidedly, "Olemaz," (This wont do,) and they would laugh and turn to something else. Everything we had was new to them, and it was often very amusing to hear them talk to each other about us.

"Do you know that these women sit at the same table with their husbands and eat with them?" said one.

"Yes, and I heard that when one of them was sick, her husband took her up and put her on the couch; then he helped make her bed, and when it was ready, he lifted her in as carefully as you would a child. Just think of our husbands doing that!"

"Oh, we are only donkeys. We do not know how to read, as these women do," said the first.

Then, in our broken Armenian, we replied, "Yes, we read God's word, this letter sent down from heaven for us all; and this is the reason why our husbands are so kind to us. Our fathers and brothers would not have consented to our coming away out here with these men, if they had not known that they too read and loved the Bible, and so would be kind to us, and care for us when we are sick, with no loving mother near."

"That is true!" said a woman, rather braver than the rest, and who, I am sure, will soon be reading for herself. We had invited our visitors this day to sit down, and Garabed, our helper, had brought in some tea in tiny little cups. It would have been considered very impolite in us not to offer some refreshment. It was their custom, and we complied with their customs when they were proper and right.

While they sat there, sipping their tea, this woman said to her next neighbor,

"I do n't believe these women are so wicked as our priests say. This one seems very gentle and kind, does n't she?"

After the tea-drinking, they go to their homes to think and talk over these things, while others come to see the house and the strange housekeeper.

"Can you work?" asks one. "Your hands look too small to do anything."

"I wish you could see her in the kitchen," says Garabed, who has just invited them into the neat sitting-room. "She can do twice as much work as I can, she knows how to do everything."

"It is because she reads," says one who looks wiser than the rest. "That is the way with these people who can read. They are not like us, only animals. She makes all her own dresses too. She does not send them to the tailor, as we do. And she can knit a stocking in a day, and it takes us a week. Have you heard of that wonderful sewing machine that some ladies in America sent to help her do her work?"

Then they must all see that wonder of wonders,

and every one wants a sample of the stitching to show some of her friends at home.

The pictures on the walls are discussed too, and some one who has visited us before says, "Do you know that is the picture of her mother-in-law? She had only one son, and she was willing that he should come out here to teach us. Ah, their religion is not like ours! I feel sure we should never do such a thing! They learn this from the Bible. The hanum (lady) says it teaches them to love others. Why did you come to this land, hanum? Do you not love your friends? I could not leave my friends, and go over so far as Bolis (Constantinople), and they say you have come much farther. Could you not get your living in your own land?"

"Oh, she is paid for coming here," says Mariam. "Don't you know she is poor, and all these things are given her for her coming here to make Protes of us? They give money to anybody who will become a Prote, our priests say, and they know."

"That's not like our Bible," pointing to one on the table, "it is the Prote Bible. Our priest has pronounced a curse on all these people. He says they are wolves in sheep's clothing; and our Bible says that just such false prophets shall come in the last days.

"These people pretend to be good, but they are only dividers of families. Have you not heard how Haji Bedros has driven his son Hohannes out of his house, because he brought home one of these Prote Bibles, and insists on reading it to his wife?"

"Did Yeghesa, his wife, go with him?" asks one of the women.

"Yes, and the Protes gave them a room, and a bed to sleep on, and sent them in food. They help all who come to them, and that is the reason why they get people to believe them. My husband came home last night, and said he would like to drive them all out of the land, for they were not only dividing families, but turning the city upside down; he heard nothing, wherever he went, but discussions about these people. Men get together in the market-places, and you would think by their noise and talk, that some great thing had happened; but it is all about these Protes. Garabed Agha, one of our chief merchants, has taken his daughter Anna home, because her husband has become a Prote. He will not let her bring her babe with her, and people say the young baby will die."

"Poor Anna!" said Nazloo; "I pity her; she must feel very sad. I wonder if she agrees with her husband; do you know, Markareed?"

"Their mother says she cries most of the time, when her father is not in the house, and wishes to go back to her husband. She says he is kinder to her than he ever was before, and she thinks he is a better man than he was when he went to hear the priest in the old church. I think you are mistaken about these people, Mariam, and if you only knew them better, you would not talk about them as you do. Besides it is not polite to talk so in the house of the hanum."

"Soos getseer, (hold your tongue,) Markareed; what do you know? Have you too become a Prote? The hanum does not understand what we are saying. Oder meg mun ay," (She is a foreigner.)

"She does understand, Mariam. Did you not see the smile on her face when you were talking? Then, as for Garabed Agha, I think he has no right to take Anna away from her husband. Kevork is a very kind man, and I know that Anna loves him a great deal better than she did before he became a Protestant. She told me she did. She says he was very unkind to her before, and seemed to think she was only a servant to wait on him. Now he says to her, 'Come, Anna, sit down and listen while I read to you out of this new book.' Even his old mother does not oppose this, but will say to her, 'Yes, come,

Annig, (little Anna,) when Kevork calls you.' This is the way these missionaries do, Mariam, and I am glad they have come to this land. I have a primer, and my husband says he will get me a Testament just as soon as I get through with my primer."

"Another Prote!" says Mariam, with a very expressive shrug of the left shoulder; "I am glad Garabed Agha has more sense than your husband has. If he had n't, our church would be destroyed by these foreigners."

"Garabed Agha will be glad enough to let Anna go back, when he finds that Kevork will not come to his terms; as he will not, for I hear they have bought a goat, and the baby is thriving on her milk. The missionaries told him to be patient, and pray over it, and God would send him back his wife in a short time. You well know, Mariam, that Garabed Agha would not long be willing to support Anna. He loves money too well for that, and it would be a greater disgrace for him to keep her than to let her go back to her husband. I do not think he would dare to give her to another man, though he says he will do so, and the priest says he will find one who will take her, as her husband has become an apostate."

But just here our Garabed came in with the

sherbet, and this put an end to the conversation between our guests. One of the little glasses is taken by each of the women except Mariam, who has been so hard on the Protestants. Garabed insisted that she should take a glass, but she refused. Markareed looked toward me, and smilingly said:

"Hanum, she is afraid to drink this, lest she too become a Prote. Some one told her that if she came to see you, you would give her sherbet, with something in it that would turn her head, and ever after she would believe just as you do; so she is determined not to drink any, though she knows it is very impolite in her not to."

You see by this story, little folks, how we became acquainted with the Armenian women, and I think you begin to understand what ignorant and strange people they were.

CHAPTER IV.

THE BEST WAY TO HELP THEM.

SUSIE is not content unless she understands everything as she goes along. And this is well, for by her questions she leads me on to say just what I want most to impress on her mind. The next talk we had she began where we left off, and the first question she asked was, "Mamma, what is sherbet? It is n't wine, is it?"

I am glad she asked me this, for perhaps some other little girl might think that we treated our visitors to wine in that country. But no; sherbet is simply a sweet drink. One kind, which is white, or of a pale green tinge, is made from a flower that grows there. It is considered very cooling and refreshing in summer; but I do not like it; it tastes something like cold tea. They have another kind which I think very pleasant to the taste. This is made of several kinds of herbs and flowers steeped together over a slow fire. They add cinnamon to it, and color it a beautiful ruby tinge, by a species of small berry which they put in just before taking it from the fire. Sugar is added after the liquid is strained, and the whole becomes a thick syrup, and is sometimes made into cakes, which are put into water when needed, and make a very nice, sweet drink. This kind is too expensive for the poor people, and is only found among the wealthier classes. Many of the people use a sour cherry, something like our cranberry, which makes a very pleasant drink; and some use only sugar and water. I have even been where they used molasses, or honey, in water.

And this starts Susie again on her questions: "Mamma, do they make molasses in Armenia? And what do they make it of? Have they sugar-cane there, or maple-trees as we have?" And she was much amused when I told her the Armenians made their molasses from mulberries and grapes.

The white mulberry is very abundant there, and is much used. It is the first fruit that ripens, and the people relish the sweet fruit after the long fast in the spring, when they have little variety in their food. When they are ripe the women bring out large sheets and spread them under the trees, which are then shaken, and the ripe fruit is easily gathered. The berries are put into a large copper boiler, a fire is kindled near the place, and the boiler is supported by large stones on each side of the fire. The fruit is cooked for several hours, and strained through a cotton bag, till all the juice is pressed out. This is put into shallow copper vessels, whitened with tin, and placed on the flat roofs of the houses, where it remains for days to evaporate in the sun. Then it is put into a narrow-necked earthen vessel, the mouth of which is covered with wet leather, and the molasses is ready. Bread-and-molasses is the morning meal of many a poor Armenian family. They also prepare a sort of sweet-meat of this molasses. They stir starch or fine flour into the fresh syrup, boil it till it becomes a paste, and then spread it on their cloth, and dry it for winter. Sometimes they put nuts upon it while it is fresh, or when it is partly dry, rolling up the nuts, strung on strings, in these thin layers. It looks very much like a sausage when rolled so. This kind of sweet paste is often brought in with the sherbet and offered to guests. I often brought home my pockets full of this *bastic*. I used to say to the kind-hearted villagers, "I cannot take so much; my pockets are full now." "Then you must bring a bag next time, as our priests do," they would say. If I refused it they would feel hurt, and would say, "Why, hanum! We have done you no honor in our house. You ate but little, and now will not take what we offer you." It was much better to take it, and then I had always something to give to the needy. So you see I had a double pleasure, that of receiving and that of giving.

There was one little girl who used to come to our house every Saturday to sweep the court. Susie remembers her very well, and that often she would fill the child's apron with these sweetmeats, and tell her to take them home to her little brothers and sisters. She was very poor. Her mother had been sick a long time, and Ater had to work hard, and often go hungry. They were not Protestants, but Ater wished to go to school and learn to read. She had no dress suitable to wear, so I told her to come and sweep the court, and earn a dress.

We might have given her a dress, but it was much better to give her work, and let her feel that she had earned it. When she had gotten this, I gave her a sacque and shoes, but if I had given her all she would not have prized them half as much. It is much better to help people to help themselves. They appreciate what they get far more if it has cost them something.

This method has been very successful in our missionary work among the Armenians. We teach them that God helps those who help themselves. When I went there, I wrote home to my friends that the poor people needed first to be clothed. I saw so many shivering in the cold, their feet looked so red, their shoes worn and their garments thin, that I longed for shiploads of warm clothing to give them. But I soon learned that if I would be a real benefactor, I must devise some way to help them help themselves, and not depend on foreign aid.

Perhaps some of you think that we could have reached their souls quicker if we had cared for the bodies. And you feel, as Susie does, that it would be nice in your little mission bands to make garments for these poor people and children, rather than make mats and tidies and iron-holders to sell at a fair. Susie said it would be "real fun" to make aprons and dresses for the bright-eyed heathen children. She even fancied she could have one little girl all to herself, and make her clothing for her. She said she believed it would stir up a missionary spirit in her, and she would want to go out and see how the little girl looked in the things. But such a plan as this would not work well.

In the first place I am not sure that the people in this country would send us the goods if we asked for them. And they would soon grow weary of it if they began. No, we go out to carry the blessed gospel to these poor people. We feel very sorry for them in all their needs; but it is better to show them how the Bible will lift them above want; not one or two of them, but the whole people, and it will also teach them to be kind to those around them who are more needy than they. I do not think we should have had so much influence over them, if we had supplied their temporal wants. We told them about the bread and water of life, and the robe of Christ's righteousness, that will never grow old.

We did not even give them the Bible. We told them they must pay something for it. If any were very poor, perhaps we would help them; but it was worth too much to them to cost them no effort to get it. Many a mother gave her jewelry, often only silver or copper, to get a Testament for her little girl. Then when she took it home, she would not give it to the baby to play with, "for she had paid for it." No, she would put a cover on it, and charge her little girl to use it with care, and not soil its clean pages.

A poor girl came to our seminary from a city three days' journey from Harpoot. Her father had hired an animal for the journey, and her mother had provided the scanty wardrobe, and a bed for her daughter. But she had no Bible, and what should she do? Should she come and ask us for the book? She must have it. She learns that she can have it for half-price. She might say to her father as he is about to leave, "Can you not give me the money for a Bible?" But that would not do, for she knows he has done all he can. So she takes out her earrings, two little gold coins, and hastens to the Bible Depository, and comes back with a shining face, with God's book in her hands, her own precious Bible. Would she have valued it so much if it had cost her nothing.

Do you say, "This was hard for the young girl; why did you not give her one?" Ah, this was a step forward in the right direction. The first step was her determination to come to school, the second her self-denial to procure her Bible, and now she was soon prepared for the third, which was giving her heart to Jesus. Now she was in a fair way to prepare herself for usefulness and happiness.

But now that I have said this, I do not wish to discourage any of the young people in America from working in their little mission circles for the heathen. There are many ways in which you can help us. This girl has come to the school with her clothes and her books, but she cannot do more.

Who will pay the expenses of the schoolhouse for her? She must be taught; who will teach her? She must be fed; who will feed her? Her father has done all he can. If not, we should say to him, "Send the money for her board and tuition also." Then who gave the Bible at half-price? Not the missionary who has only enough for his own wants, and often needs the help of friends to pay the expenses of his own children at school in the homeland. Your mission circles, and the friends who would be so willing to fill the boxes with garments for the bodies of these poor people, must help pay these bills which they cannot. So do all you can, little girls, dear young ladies; there never was greater need than now. But instead of garments which will wear out, send them the Bible, and food for the mind and soul. Their degradation and poverty will flee before this as the mists of the morning disappear before the bright sun. If you raise thirty dollars, you can keep a girl in the seminary a whole year; or, for a little more, you can sustain a school a year in some village, where one of the girls educated in the seminary may go, to teach forty or fifty children to read the Bible.

Then there are Bible-readers, as we call them, who go from house to house to teach the women to read. They cannot do this unless they are paid for it, any more than teachers in the schools. They must eat and drink as we do, and I assure you they earn the money we give them. Some of them are real missionaries, and endure great self-denial to do this work.

I wish I could take your mission circle into the village where one of our girls is teaching, and show you her work. I feel quite sure you would think it paid for you to go once in two weeks to the circle, to work on mats, tidies, or even iron-holders, if in this way you can get money to support Lizzie, while she is trying to do good in these dark homes. I think you would say, "We must have more girls come to our circle, so that we can raise money enough for a school in more than this one village." And there are hundreds of such villages where we can work.

So work away, all of you who can. You are just as much needed as the missionaries themselves. They are only helpers; so are you. You have perhaps never thought you could do so much. Hereafter then you will look upon your work at home very differently, I think. You see it is not to dress up these poor children, as you would your dolls, but to prepare them to be noble men and women, and true Christians. If you can support a band of teachers to open schools in these dark and degraded villages, from them will go out thousands, who in their turn will educate others, and so the work will go on, until the whole world shall become like "the garden of the Lord."

Jesus said that not even a cup of cold water given in his name, from love to him, should go unrewarded. The smallest child in any missionary circle can give and do something, and Jesus, the Great Treasurer, will keep the account. It will all be safely kept in Heaven's Savings Bank, and when our work is all done, and we go to live with Jesus in his beautiful home in heaven, we shall find it all there, with a great deal of interest added.

CHAPTER V.

THE VILLAGE-SCHOOL TEACHER.

It would give me great pleasure if I could introduce Susie, and all the dear young friends of the mission bands in the home land, to Yeghesa, or Lizzie, and her school in her native village. We would go first to the place where we found her; we cannot honor it with the name of home, for we find nothing there that seems like home, excepting the Bible which she has already obtained.

We enter the low, narrow door by stooping. We think this cannot be the place where a family lives, but must be an outside room where they are cooking; for, it being only ten o'clock in the morning, or the fourth hour, as they reckon, the smoke from their breakfast has not all escaped through the hole in the roof, and the little window, a foot square in the side. Lizzie's mother rises to greet us, then places a cushion near the fireplace for us to sit upon. Chairs, sofas, and divans are unknown in these village houses. It is a cold morning, and we are invited to put our feet into the fireplace and warm them. I say *into*, for the fireplace

looks much like a small well. It is a hole in the earth, three or four feet deep, and stoned about the sides, much as our farmers make stone walls around their fields. In the morning grass and brush are brought, and a fire kindled, upon which are placed cakes of prepared wood, or what we call village peat.

Those tired unhappy-looking women, with great baskets on their shoulders, whom we met as we rode into the village, were going after a supply of this fuel. The baskets they carried were full of manure which they take to a hole outside the village. They pour in water, add a little chopped straw or grass, and then a number of the women—brides they are called because they are married—get in and trample it with their bare feet until it is well mixed. Then with their hands they make it into flat cakes, and put it in a sunny place to dry. When it is thoroughly dried they pack it in their baskets to take home. This way of preparing fuel is probably as old as Bible times.

The village houses have but one room, which serves as parlor, kitchen, bedroom, and storeroom; and if they are rich enough to own cattle, as stable also. But Lizzie's mother is too poor for cattle, and her parlor had little in it except smoke. The walls are black and shiny, like the inside of a chimney that has been used for years.

When I first went to see this family the mother had been weeping. She held the Bible in her hand. We had a Bible woman in this village, and she had visited this poor woman, and had taught her to read. She was in great sorrow at this time for her husband had just died, and she refused to be comforted. She had no hope that he had gone to be with the blessed Saviour. She felt too that that she was a stranger to that dear Jesus who died upon the cross to redeem her. I took the Bible and read how Jesus had gone to his Father's house in the heavenly city, to prepare mansions for those who love him and keep his commandments. I told her that Jesus said he would come again, and take her to that blissful abode, and that God would be her Father, if she would love and serve him. She cannot help her husband now, but she can train up her three fatherless children to be Christians; her Heavenly Father has given her this great work to do for him.

My interest in this poor woman made me forget the dark, gloomy room and the black walls. Even the smoke ceased to trouble me. As we talked, I became interested in her daughter Lizzie. I thought how useful she might become, if she could only have the advantages of the seminary at Harpoot. I proposed that she should go there, and both mother and daughter were delighted with the idea; but how could she? She had but one dress, that which she had on. It was made of a coarse blue cloth, woven in the rude looms of her native village. Now is the time for us to help her help herself; but how shall we do it?

I know what you are thinking of, little folks. You are thinking of those boxes of ready-made clothes we were talking about yesterday, which the mission bands ought to make and send across the sea. But let us talk with this mother and daughter first, and see how much they can do.

"You would like to have Lizzie go up to Harpoot to school. You are poor, and we will give her board and tuition, and perhaps some one will help her get the books she will need; but what will she do for clothing and a bed? Can you provide them?"

"I think I can, Hanum. I have enough blue cloth to make her a dress, and red enough to make an apron to trim it. I will wash the one she has on, and mend it nicely, and she can wear it to work in." She understood that the girls at the school do their own work.

"Then I have a new handkerchief, or veil," she continued, "which was given to me, which will do for her head. She can take my stockings, and I will wear her father's. One of my neighbors has a little money, which my husband lent him, and this will get her some shoes, and help about her books. The man said he would give it to me as soon as he had sold his cotton, and I hear he has gone to the city with a load to-day.

"I will take her father's bed and quilt down to the fountain and wash them, and make them over, and they will be as good as new. Then I will take the towels that were given to me when I was a bride, and Lizzie will be ready in a few days to go to school. I think my neighbor Kevork will take her up to the city, as he goes quite often."

Now wasn't that much better than to have given her a complete outfit?

In due time the village-girl appeared in the court of the mission-house. Do not laugh though she is mounted on a mule astride her bed and baggage. Some girls have to take their baggage on their shoulders and walk to school.

Miss Pond, the young lady who has come out from America to teach the girls, receives Lizzie very kindly, and inquires for her mother in such a way as to cheer the stranger girl's heart. She feels sure from that moment, that she shall love this teacher, who has left her friends and come to a far-off land to teach such a poor girl as she is.

The bell rings, and the pupils come flocking into the school. The city girls give her a kindly glance. Her dress is not like theirs, but it is new, and a goodly number from the villages are dressed just as she is. She is rough-looking, and awkward, and she feels it.

She reads her verse from the Testament with a trembling voice, and in the opening prayer the teacher remembers the new pupil, and asks God to bless and help her every day while in the school, and make her useful when she goes back to the village among her own people. After devotions, Miss West assigns her lessons, and she begins her school-life.

Seven happy months pass away, and we enter the schoolroom again. It has been swept with more than usual care, and some pieces of carpet spread on one side. The desks have been removed, and chairs brought in for expected guests. The teachers at their desks are on the south side of the room, and all the schoolgirls, dressed in their best, are seated on the floor at their left hand. The women are coming in aud quietly taking their seats on the carpets, and the invited guests, friends of the pupils, occupy the chairs. It is a select company, for it is a girls' school, and here in Turkey, at this time, it will not do to admit any gentlemen but the fathers of the girls, to see their uncovered faces. Even their brothers are excluded.

And now we will look for Lizzie. Can it be possible that nice-looking girl in the neat pink calico dress is she? It looks like her face, but she has grown whiter and handsomer. The little black handkerchief is tied tastefully over her nicely-braided hair, and her purple merino jacket is very becoming to her. What have the teachers done to her? you will ask; or perhaps you will conclude that some one has sent her a box at last.

But no, she has had no help from others. Her mother worked in the fields to get this new dress and jacket for her daughter, that she might look more like the other girls. We are glad she has them, but it is much better that her friends should get them, than that they should be given to her by others. She has been an earnest scholar, has studied hard; and better than all, we think she has truly become a follower of the Lord Jesus. This new love in her heart, with the clean rooms and good food up here at the school, and her new dress, account for the great change in her appearance.

And now examination is over, and vacation begins. Lizzie is going to teach school in her native village, and board at home. What! in that dark, smoky room, all this long vacation, with that dirty-looking mother and brother and sister? Yes: We shall give her a small sum, from one to two dollars a month, at the most, and in this way she can help herself, and at the same time help us to elevate the little girls in that village.

Her schoolroom is very uninviting. She has resumed her blue village dress, and finds it hard to keep herself looking tidy, but she does, and she has a great influence over the little girls. They look up to her with great respect, for she has been up to Harpoot to be taught by those wise teachers who came from over the sea.

All winter Lizzie works faithfully, and in the spring is found among the happy "old scholars" who come flocking back to the school, as doves to their windows. She came a day or two in advance, to help make the home cheerful for the new-comers. She wears the neat, pink dress, which has been worn only on great occasions during the winter. Her face has lost some of its brightness, and her hands look as if water had not been very abundant. She has the smell of smoke about her, the real peat smell, which makes us open our windows after we have had guests from houses where that fuel is used. But this will soon pass away in our pure Harpoot air. Her appetite is good after a long winter, when meat has seldom been seen, and the diet extremely plain. She relishes study too, and seems more in earnest than ever before. The new scholars look up to her as a leader, and she is careful to set the best example before them.

Her voice is heard in the daily prayer-meeting, and sometimes you may see her in earnest conversation with some new scholar, and it is easy to see that she is talking with them about the dear Saviour she wishes them to love as she does.

The three years she designed to stay at the seminary pass thus pleasantly away, and Lizzie is busy with a new dress for graduation. This too is of calico, and the purple sack is to be changed for one of green. Her hair is put back under a black silk net of her own making; the worms which spun the silk, having, perhaps, been fed by her mother's hands. A small crocheted collar, fastened by a bow of bright ribbon, gives a finish to her dress.

Lizzie is by no means the best scholar in her

class, for one of her classmates is beautiful Azneev, who will read us a composition on "Female Responsibility," that would do honor to any young lady in an American school. And there are others who will surpass Lizzie in higher branches, but she will do well in all the common studies, and no one could help being interested in her examination in the Bible. She will not fail in this, but be ready for whatever question may be put to her. The deacon of the little church in her native village— for a church has been formed there, and they have begun to support their pastor—comes up to the seminary at this time to engage Lizzie for the girls' school.

We say, "Deacon Hohannes, we cannot give Lizzie to you this winter."

He is much disturbed by this, and wishes to know our reason. "Surely, hanum, you will not put Lizzie in any other village! She belongs to us. What do you mean?"

"We have sent Lizzie to you for two years," we answer, "and she has spent the winters in that dark, dirty home with her mother. She has now graduated, and is a nice, neat girl, and we wish her to keep herself so, and she cannot do this in such a home. We will put her where she can. There are other places where she can teach, and be in a pleasant family, for she is one of our most reliable girls."

"Why, hanum, we will go home and build a room for her in her mother's house, if you will help us a very little. Give us only five dollars, and we will pay all the other expenses."

We told him we would give it when the room was fitted up, for this was just what we wished them to do. We knew they could not do the whole. The people of that village, Hoghi, are very poor, and most of the houses are like that of Lizzie's mother; and the people were doing all they could for their pastor and their boys' school.

They at once went to work, and soon had a little room with two windows in it ready, on the roof of her mother's house. They whitened its mud-walls with a clay-wash, put a reed-carpet on the floor, and came up to the city to buy a sheet-iron stove to put in it. The first stoves in Harpoot were imported by the missionaries. Now the city has two rival manufactories of sheet-iron stoves. They are yet unable to melt iron for casting.

We gladly gave the deacon the five dollars we had promised, and Lizzie for their teacher. The room and stove did a great deal of good in that vil-

lage, and now we find other rooms quite as comfortable. Deacon Hohannes has a cheerful sitting-room, with a stove in it, and a carpet on the floor, and cushions to sit on at the sides of the room, so that one can lean back against the wall. His wife and mother are pupils of the earnest Bible-woman, one of our very best, a native of the same village, and also educated in our seminary at Harpoot; and Hohannes, his son, is preparing, in the Harpoot Normal School, to be a teacher or preacher.

I think it will pay for the little girls and young ladies in America to educate teachers like these. Susie is ready to do her part, and she has come to the conclusion that it is better for them to get their own clothes, while she and her friends send money for the schools. She sees too, how, as these girls are educated, they begin at once to improve their persons and their homes, and to gather about them the comforts of civilization.

CHAPTER VI.

MARIAM, THE HOGHI BIBLE-WOMAN.

The work of a Bible-woman in Armenia is not merely to go from house to house, to read the Bible to the women, and pray with them. We have found that, unless we get the women to help themselves, they make little or no progress. The most of the women in the Harpoot villages are willing that the clean, nice-looking Bible-women should come in and read, and even pray with them, and then some of them would make the sign of the cross, and exclaim, "Yes, God is merciful! Salvation is free! Blessed be the Lord!" We do not believe in the piety that consists alone in pious exclamations; we therefore test their zeal by setting them at work. If we can persuade them to buy a primer and begin their A, B, C's, we feel that we have gained an influence over them that will tend to elevate them, and bring them out of their present wretchedness into the blessings of a Christian civilization. For the primer is called "the key to unlock the Bible," and this opens the way to Christian civilization. We never get a woman through the primer, who is not anxious to have a Testament. Indeed, this is the strong inducement we hold out to her, when, with great difficulty, she spells out the hard words in her primer. Many a woman falters, and seems ready to give up before she gets through the first few pages of her lesson-book, and then we turn over a few leaves to some simple passage of Scripture, and let her read it with our help, and assure her if she patiently goes on, she will soon be reading God's book.

The Bible-woman has to give this lesson, explain it to her, and then, kneeling with her, ask God to help her understand it. If she prays over her lesson, she will learn it, even though her home be a dark one, and she may have to hold one baby in her arms, and pull the string fastened to the hammock that contains another.

I wish I could take all the dear young people at home, and all the Christian mothers who love to have their children work for the heathen, into some of these homes, where they have for ages heard the name of Christ, and believed that he died for them, and yet are more cheerless than many a heathen one. They have no comforts, but just drag out a miserable existence. The only thing that can elevate them is the light and knowledge of the Bible, the thrice-blessed Bible.

Our Bible-woman Mariam, or Mary, like Lizzie, came from a dark and degraded home; but the light of God's word entered the dwelling, and her father, Sarkis, received it into his heart, and became an earnest follower of the Saviour. We soon saw the fruit of this conversion. He had three daughters. He was poor, but he came up to Harpoot, and asked that the eldest might be admitted to the seminary. She was "only a girl," but the father was so changed by his conversion to a living Christianity, that he became really in earnest to have his daughter educated.

The fact that he wished this was a good evidence of the change in the father, for, in Armenia, girls are looked upon almost with contempt, and it is not only thought unnecessary to educate them, but some parents are strongly opposed to it. "They can do what is required of them without an education," it is said, "and will be far more obedient. Their mothers and husbands' mothers were not educated, and why should our girls be? It will only lift them out of their place, and make them impudent and lazy."

But Sarkis brought Mariam to the school, and

provided her with clothes and books, and gave about one-fourth of the money required for other expenses. This was making a great effort, and he seemed very happy in doing it. And yet, had you seen him, you would have said, "He looks more like a beggar himself, than a man who can pay part of his daughter's expenses at school." It is true his garments were very coarse and old, but this very effort to help his daughter tended to elevate himself.

A few months passed away, and this father came to visit the daughter at school; and this time he brought his wife, Mariam's mother, with him. Each was dressed in a new suit of village-blue, and looked very neat and respectable. Nor did they come empty-handed. The daughter had her parcel from home, and the teachers theirs, as a token of respect. And the missionary families were not forgotten. A few eggs, a pail of sour milk, or some cucumbers, were given to each. These little "love-tokens," as they call them, were gratefully received. They did not throw themselves on the hospitality of teachers or missionaries, but brought their food with them, and went to the house of an acquaintance in the city, where they asked permission for Mariam to spend the Sabbath with them.

We could not ask them to stay at the seminary. We had neither room nor means for the crowds who would wish to come if we had offered to entertain them. Six days out of each week the friends of our pupils could call upon us, at any hour of the day, and we always received them kindly and politely; but never on the Sabbath unless in extraordinary cases. From the first we taught them that the Sabbath was a holy day, and it was better for them to go to the place of worship, and then read and meditate in their own homes, and with their own families. This training was all the more necessary, from the fact that the Sabbath had been to them little more than a holiday, when they might go from house to house to gossip, or have more time for a good dinner.

We did not even allow them to come to us for religious conversation on Sunday, when we were in the city, except in special cases; but when we were in the villages our room was open to any who might come, and it was a religious service all day. Often the only suitable place to be found was the room used as a chapel, and we were generally very weary, when, late in the evening, the last man had left. Perhaps there are some who will think we lost a great opportunity of doing good in the city by not encouraging their visits on Sunday. But we did not seek what would bring the greatest crowds about us, but what would be the best way of planting a Bible Christianity among the people.

They sometimes came to us for tea, sugar or wood, and had we given all they wished, we should soon have found our own stores empty, and only "a bread and cheese work," as one missionary expressed it, to show for it. We did give delicacies to the sick, and, according to our ability, remembered the poor about us. And we taught them in many temporal things besides. We were often asked to cut and fit dresses and sacques like ours, but seldom did it. We had a more important work to do than to be dressmakers. Their style of dress was neat, and, as we thought, more becoming to them than ours. We were willing to give them patterns, and show them how to do these things for themselves; our time was thus saved, and our patience spared, and the lesson they learned was far more lasting than it otherwise could have been. Had we fitted and made the dresses, they would probably have found fault with them, and demanded to have them made in some other way.

But to return to Mariam. She finished her seminary course of study, and then took lessons in another school, where the Master intended she should graduate, that she might be still better prepared for the work he had for her to do.

One bright morning pastor Mardiros came in to see Miss Pond, seeming more than usually thoughtful. He inquired if she thought Mariam would make a good wife for Mr. Geragos, who was about to graduate from the Theological Seminary. This was very unexpected to us all, but after some consultation the consent of the teachers and missionaries was obtained, and a friend was sent to ask permission of the father and mother. Of course it made quite a stir in that quiet village home, and the young man was thoroughly discussed. He was from the city of Palu, and bore a good name there, and was of more than ordinary talent. Indeed, he was so energetic that he paid his own way while in the seminary. At times he had been under great mental depression, but it seemed more like a spiritual than a physical trouble. The parents gave consent, and it was decided that the wedding festivities should be at the close of the fall term of school, and in the girl's schoolroom, she being the first one to be married from the first graduating class of our new Female Seminary.

But I had almost forgotten to tell you about the

betrothal, which occurred in this case only a few weeks before marriage, though sometimes years intervene.

You would have been amused perhaps, if you had seen Geragos when he came into the Bible Depository, and asked for one of the best red-covered, gilt-edged Bibles, worth about three dollars. He was careful to see that it was perfect, and the very best to be had. On the blank leaf was written the betrothal pledge. Then with some extra attention to his usually neat attire, he was ready for the evening, that seemed a long way off, although it was now past four o'clock.

Miss Pond had asked that tea be served a little earlier than usual, as the betrothal was to be in her sittingroom. Some extra lamps made the room more cheerful, the missionary families were invited in, and the schoolgirls were present. All things were ready at seven, and the pastor accompanied by Geragos, made his appearance. Mariam was seated between Miss Pond and Kohar, the assistant teacher. Kohar with Mariam went forward and made the usual salutation, and all the girls followed. When they were again seated, pastor Mardiros read a portion of Scripture and prayed, and a hymn was sung. Then taking the Bible from the table he went forward towards the parties to be betrothed, and said a few words on the sacredness of the pledge they were about to make to each other; and handing the Bible to Mariam, said, "By accepting this you pledge yourself to be the future wife of Geragos." She rose and modestly accepted the Bible, and Geragos put a ring on her finger. After this we sang once more, and tea and cake were served, after which Kohar and Mariam, rising, made the usual salutation and left the room, the schoolgirls following in the same manner. The young bridegroom elect was congratulated, and after a few pleasant words, he left with the pastor.

Mariam was at that time probably about seventeen years of age, but we had to judge from her appearance. Armenian mothers are very apt to forget the ages of their children. We are careful now to furnish records in their Bibles, and to instruct them to have the names of their children and the dates of their birth written.

It is the usual custom to have a wedding take place at the house of the bridegroom's father, but in Mariam's case we took the liberty to arrange otherwise. The father of Geragos was dead, and his mother opposed to his being a Protestant, or marrying one. It is usual too for the bridegroom to furnish the wedding dress; but as Geragos had no friends to make it, pastor Mardiros' wife, Heripsima, acted the part of sister and made it for him. It was a Turkish silk, and the colors were green, yellow, and red. It was quite pretty, and with a neat jacket of green broadcloth, and a light gauze head-dress, Mariam looked very pretty on the evening of the wedding.

Some friends of Geragos and some also of the bride were invited. The girls carpeted the schoolroom with rugs, and when well-lighted it looked very cheerful. A long table with refreshments was so arranged between the central pillars of the room as to give a pleasing effect to the whole.

All things being ready, the bridegroom and his friends went with lanterns to the house of pastor Mardiros, and escorted the bride and her attendants to the schoolroom with songs of rejoicing. The ceremony was nearly an hour long, and parts of it very original, but even the most fastidious could not say it was incomplete in any respect. The good things with which the table was spread soon disappeared, and the company quietly went to their homes. The pastor had invited the bridegroom to make his house their home for a few days till he should take his bride to see her friends in Hoghi, before entering on his work of preaching in a large village not far from Harpoot.

A few days later the bride called to bid us good-by before leaving the city, and we thought her very lady-like and pretty in her new position. We sent her away with many good wishes for her future, little knowing how trying it would be. The mental depression we had known of in his seminary days increased upon Geragos until he became insane. Some thought it unsafe for Mariam to stay stay with him, but she would never leave him except to go to a near neighbor's to rest for a night. When she was away from him he would call after her, and beg her not to leave him with others. He would use the harshest language to others but never to her.

It was very touching to see her leading him in the streets when he insisted on going abroad. While others were afraid of, and shunned him, she could always quiet him. Her beautiful little girl of two years was taken from her to the heavenly home, and Mariam was indeed sorely afflicted. Her father took them home, and after several months Geragos was so much better that he sought work. They were very poor, and it was at this time that Mariam began her labors as our Hoghi Bible-woman. She had a little babe only a few months old. After the breakfast was over, and her husband had gone to his work, she would take her babe in her arms, and go from house to house to give lessons to the women. We had regular written reports of her labors, and were pleased with the success that seemed to crown her efforts.

Another day I will tell my young friends of a visit I made to Hoghi to examine Mariam's pupils, and you will all better understand her work.

CHAPTER VII.

VISIT TO HOGHI.

As my young readers in America cannot go with me to Hoghi to see what the Bible-woman is doing there, I have no doubt they will be pleased with an account of the visit Susie and I made in that poor village; poor indeed and miserable in its appearance, yet with many immortal souls, more precious than gold, to be won to Christ.

Garabed is at the door, and sends in word that the animals are ready for us.

"What have you in those great leather bags, mamma?" said Susie. "They are large enough for us to ride in; but I hope we are not to go in that fashion, are we?"

"No, my dear; we cannot spare the *hoorges* for you or me; you can ride on the white donkey, and I will take the mule. We need the hoorges to put our beds and some cooking utensils in; and we will take some food with us, for we shall not find much that we can eat in the village. Besides, the people are poor, and we do not wish to be burdensome to them."

"But where are we going to stay, mamma?"

"I think the pastor will let us have his little study."

It was winter, and we dressed ourselves warmly, especially our feet, as we were to be two or three hours on the way, and the winds from the mountains were cold and chilling. As we rode into the village, and saw the people looking so poor and cold, and the houses like mud huts, Susie exclaimed, "O mamma, I am so glad I was not born in one of those houses, that I am not one of these little village-girls!"

"So am I," I answered; "but, my child, it is only the Bible that makes us to differ. These Armenians are just as capable of a Christian civilization as we are, and it is to bring this that we have come to them. It is a blessed work God has given to the Christians in our happy America, to send this Bible to the millions that have it not; and it is a great privilege to be permitted to bring it."

We did not go out that day, but permitted the people to call upon us; and after seeing some of them, and planning with Mariam about the calls we should make in the morning, we decided to go into the prayer-meeting which was to be held in the chapel that evening.

Susie was quite amused at the idea of sitting on the floor with the women, but I told her I always did, only they usually gave me a cushion to sit upon.

"I think the pastor will have one carried in for us, Susie; and the people will be delighted to see us. I always enjoy a village tour. It seems to me more like the work Jesus did when he came down from his beautiful home in heaven. It is more like that than our work in the city."

There is a great difference between the city and the villages; and the villages differ very much from each other. In Hoghi the Bible-work had then made more progress among the women, than in any other, and we had reason to believe that those wretched homes would ere long be exchanged for light, cheerful and cleanly abodes. The pastor's cheerful sitting-room was a model, and that of Deacon Hohannes, which we stepped across the narrow street to see, Susie thought even more pleasant. Yet when we first knew him he lived in a cellar-room. The gospel has brought him up into the second story, has brought him these cushions, the coarse carpet, that little stove, and, better than all, a neat bookcase filled with books. Yes, and it is this which makes his pretty little wife look so bright and intelligent. She is one of Mariam's best scholars.

Susie thought her really beautiful in her clean blue and red village dress, with a neat bib-apron.

When we returned to the pastor's, we found that Garabed had made a fire, and put up our little bedsteads, and the room looked more cheerful and homelike than before. Our beds are a missionary invention, designed for comfort in going from place to place, as we cannot safely sleep on the earth-floor. They weigh, sack and all, only about ten pounds, and can be folded up like an umbrella, so as to be easily carried.

We did not pass a very quiet night, however, for the dogs that abound in that region, both in city and village, make the night hideous with their howls. They are only street dogs and have no owners, and the villagers are accustomed to their noise. They never kill them, unless they fear they have become mad. And there is no sleep in the morning for the early cock-crowing. These domestic fowls are the only clocks these poor people have. We heed their call and rise promptly, that we may fold up our beds and put them in the leather bags and convert our sleeping-room into a parlor again; and then we are ready for breakfast.

Garabed brought in the breakfast on the pastor's round copper table, which you would call a tray, and placed it on a low stool. The tin box was opened, and with some coffee and warm milk we made a good repast. We then repaired to the pastor's room for prayers. Susie thought it would be pleasanter to be alone in our own snug little room for devotions, but I reminded her that we did not come here to please ourselves. I knew that many of the villagers, knowing we were there, would esteem it a privilege to come in. We were then ready to start on our visiting with Mariam, who soon appeared with her baby in her arms.

"I have to take my little one when I go to give my lessons," she said, "for I fear to leave her with her father, as he is not perfectly sane now. I get very tired, but I love my work."

"How many pupils have you now?" I asked.

"Sixty; and I give thirty lessons each day. These keep me very busy. After I have finished my round, I go to the sunset prayer-meeting, and then home to prepare our evening meal."

"Does not Geragos help you?"

"Perhaps he will have a fire in the little stove, when I get home, and perhaps not."

"Have you a stove?"

"Yes, hanum; we have a tiny sheet-iron stove with a hole in the top for a kettle, and I can do all my cooking there very nicely. We live very simply. Sometimes it is cracked wheat, with a little pemmican (prepared meat) added to give it a relish, or a mixed soup, which perhaps you would n't like; or pulse, such as the prophet Daniel fared so well on. It does n't take much time to get our food."

We did our talking as we went along, for I wanted Susie to know how Mariam lived and worked. Soon we were at Markareed's house.

"We have come, Markareed," we said, "to hear you read, and see what progress you have made."

She timidly brought out her primer and spelled out the hard words; the easy ones she had learned to pronounce without spelling. We questioned her a little, and found that with Mariam's explanation, she had quite a good idea of the simple story she read; but she said, "Hanum, it is very hard for me. If my husband did not encourage me, and say, 'See how nicely teacher Mariam reads; she had to read the primer first, as she told you,' I should give up, I know I should."

"But are there not hundreds of women in this village," we asked, "whose husbands treat them like donkeys, and when they ask for a primer tell them to shut their mouths, for a woman has no brains? You ought to be thankful, Markareed, that your husband wants you to learn."

We left her with a song of gratitude in her mouth, though her home looked so wretched we could not help feeling all the while a pity for her. Yet we knew that all she needed was encouragement to help herself. Her husband, who is a member of the Hoghi church, will soon have as comfortable a home as Deacon Hohannes has. Markareed has more intellect than the deacon's wife, but she is not so sweet-tempered. We pray that she may truly love Jesus, as her husband does, and then she will be more patient in learning to read.

In the next house we visited we were obliged to step carefully, for the passage-way was very dark, and in some places, Mariam said, the floor was broken. We at last reached a large room where men and women were at work pulling cotton out of the pods, and passing it through a simple machine to free it from the seeds. Our greeting here was cordial indeed. "Good morning, hanum; we are glad to see you. Welcome! a thousand times welcome! Why did not the badvellie (minister) come too? Is this your little girl? Sara, bring some better cushions, quick! Put one under her feet. Sit down here, little girl. Can you read? What's your name?"

"Susie," I answered for the child; "in your language it is Shushig."

"Shushig, Shushig, come here, karnoog, (lambkin,) and sit by me," said a very old lady, the grandmother and great-grandmother of this patriarchal family, whose name was Nana.

"I see your hands are all busy," I said; "and how do you succeed in learning to read?"

"Oh, they can all read but me," replied the grandmother. "Even these bits of children go to Lizzie's school, and come home knowing more than their old Nana. I wish it had come in my day, but my old eyes can't see now. I can only listen, but I thank God every day that he has been so kind to my house. I thank him for that blessed Bible that Kevork reads to us every night and morning."

"Do you think your son is a better man now that he reads the Bible?"

"Oh yes, hanum, we are all better. Mariam—the Lord bless her!—is doing a good work here. I wish all my brides to read. They will be better women, and do more work."

We next entered a small house with only one room. The mother met us at the door, and we went in and took our seats on an old cushion beside the fireplace, where the evening meal was cooking. "Will you put your feet in and warm them?" she said, as she lifted a dingy-looking cloth, and moved the earthen cover of the oven aside. A little girl of four years sat near by, without shoes or stockings. Something moved in a hammock swung across the other corner of the room, and the woman reaching forward, caught a string suspended from it, and swung it back and forth until the motion of the bunch of rags within ceased. This young mother has a bright, pretty face.

"Can she read?" we inquired.

"Bring your Bible, Anna," said Mariam, "and turn to the fifty-first of Isaiah, and read."

She took her book from a box, and read very correctly, asking several questions about God's ancient people. She seemed to love the Bible, and we can but hope that its light will never go out in this humble home. She asked us to pray with her, and we earnestly commended her to the dear Saviour, who, when he was on earth, delighted to visit the poor and needy. She followed us to the door, and urged us to come again.

CHAPTER VIII.

LIGHT IN DARK HOMES.

Continuing our calls, we entered a court, around which were houses of a better class than those we had visited. But a sound as of quarrelling saluted us as we approached, and Mariam, ascending a flight of steps, motioned us to stop till she could ascertain the trouble. She soon returned and asked us to follow.

"I have a pupil here, hanum," she said, "but I fear she will not be able to take a lesson to-day, for they have just had a serious quarrel. Loosig is a young bride, and her husband is the only Protestant in the family. The uncle is enraged about it, but Loosig's father-in-law stands up for his son, and says he has a right to be a Protestant if he wishes, and Loosig shall read if her husband is willing."

As we entered, Loosig and her father-in-law rose to greet us, and the young woman brought us a cushion; but the others only looked at us with dark, scowling faces. They would have told us to leave, but they were afraid of Loosig's father-in-law, and so kept still. We hardly knew what to do, but concluded to try the efficacy of kind words. So we said to the eldest of these women,

"Sister Noonig, as Mariam goes from house to house to give the sisters lessons, would you not like to learn?"

In reply, Noonig was violent and abusive. She cursed "the hateful Protes," who had come to be "dividers of families," and derisively said, "Why don't you go to the Turks? We are Christians, as well as you. We do not wish the Prote Bible; it only makes people worse."

"It is just like yours in the church, Noonig, only it is in a language you can understand. If you would read this beautiful letter God has sent you, you would not curse us or any one. This book teaches us to love even our enemies, and pray for those who are unkind to us. I think you are unhappy because you do not read and love this book."

"I have to work for my living; so do my brides. You, who live in the city, have nothing to do; you keep servants to do your work. Look at your small, white hands. I cannot wear broadcloth"—pointing to my waterproof dress—"my garments are only cotton. Then this Bible-woman is paid for giving lessons. Pay me, and I will work."

You will readily perceive the ignorance of this poor woman. We have to be patient with such, and though we do not answer all they say, we do sometimes think it worth while to make some explanations. So I said:

"Noonig, sister, we all have to work for our living. Even those you call rich do more than you give them credit for. Come to the city, and see me in my own house. I have only one woman to help me, and my house has six rooms to be put in order each day. We have three meals, while you have only two; we do our own sewing, which you know is much more than yours; we have many guests, go out to call and instruct the people, teach in the school, and our own children, too, as we have no schools for them, hold prayer-meetings and mothers' meetings, visit the sick, and do many other things beside. Now your wants are few, and you have five strong women in this house. Yet you do not keep it neat, and your own garments are dirty—"

"Who could keep clean in such a house as this?" interrupted Noonig. "I hear that your house is very fine, and you do not fight as we do."

"The reason of that is that we read the Bible; and that is what we want you to do Good Christian people from America have opened a school up in Harpoot, where your Bible-woman was taught, and now we give her enough to buy her bread, so that she can come here and teach you and your brides. Do you not think she earns what we give her?"

"Yes; they say she goes about with that baby in her arms from morning till night, and her husband at home crazy. She has grown pale and thin, poor thing. Everybody speaks well of her, and of Geragos too, for he is kind."

"If you would learn to read, Noonig, perhaps your husband and brother would learn too, and your home would be much happier."

"Would it bring me a better house?"

"Yes, I think it would. If I had not read and obeyed this blessed book, I might be just as wretched as you are. Shall I read you a little out of my Bible?" taking my little Testament from my pocket. I opened to Christ's Sermon on the Mount, and read a few verses.

"Hear this," I said; "'Blessed are the peacemakers, for they shall be called the children of God.' God loves the peacemakers. I think he would like to have some here in your house. Why are you not a peacemaker here?" I asked, turning to Atam (Adam) the father-in-law.

"These women quarrel all the time," he replied, "and it needs my cane to keep them straight. I hear you do not believe in beating the women, but what should we do with them without a cane? They are nothing but children. I mean to defend Loosig, and let her read, and we will see if she is any better for it."

"But you will need the Bible," I said; "listen again to the word, 'Blessed are the pure in heart, for they shall see God.'"

"*See God*, hanum! What does that mean?"

"It means that if we are pure, as he is, we shall live with him in heaven."

"Hanum, if you will persuade my wife to learn to read, I will buy her all the books she needs, and when she learns to read the Testament, I will buy her one with a red cover and gilt edges; do you hear that, Juhar?" addressing a quiet little woman who had not ventured to open her lips.

"Atam," I said, "are you not the eldest brother in this house?"

"Yes."

"Why, then, does Noonig, your younger brother's wife, seem to be the head among the brides?"

"Juhar is my second wife, and Noonig is older, and much more capable. If you can only persuade her to read, all the rest will follow; but they are afraid of her."

Yes, Noonig has a high position in this house, and a great responsibility is resting upon her. I fear she will be speechless when she stands before the Great Judge, and he asks why she did not do her duty by her household.

But now Loosig, the timid young bride of fifteen, came shyly along to take her lesson. After that was over we united in a short prayer, and even Noonig was softened enough to bow her head and listen. She rose when we left, and bade us go in peace, and we went away feeling sure that her icy haughtiness would melt away before the power of the gospel, which has already begun to be felt in that home. Loosig means *little light*, and we trust the true light is to shine through her and dispel the darkness. May we not hope that Atam, whose name means *man*, will rise to a noble manhood, and Juhor, *jewel*, will shine as the stars for ever?

"I wish you would go in here; I have no pupil here, but they need light," said Mariam, as we came to another house.

We followed her, feeling somewhat afraid, for

as the outer door was opened, and we looked in, we saw that we had to pass close by some buffalo-oxen, which seemed to fill the front entry, and we did not fancy being so near these ugly-looking creatures. The buffaloes in that land are large, horned animals, considerable larger, and far less docile than our oxen, and well calculated to frighten timid people. But with Mariam for our guide, we went on into the family drawingroom. A village drawingroom! and we find many such in Armenia.

There was a stone fireplace on one side of the apartment, but it was quite too dark to see whether those who were sitting beside it were men or women. They did not rise to greet us, at all events, for we were "only women." We soon found, however, from their voices, that there were men there, and they were smoking their pipes. Two or three women then came forward and gave us a seat at the right of the fireplace, and Mariam said,

"I have brought the hanum to see you."

"*Paree yegar*," (you come in peace,) all exclaimed at once, and the men asked, "Is it the hanum, the badvellic's wife?"

We heard the cattle munching their straw, and when we "got our eyes," as the Armenians say, when going into a dark place, we saw that the room was only one corner of the great stable, with a low railing around it. We knew this family must be in quite comfortable circumstances, from the number of animals, and also from the fact that both men and women were persons of leisure. We saw none of the wheels or looms or cotton we had seen in the other houses. The women in this house have work enough in taking care of the cattle, making peat, and cooking the meals. The men in such a family do the gossiping, or "spin street yarn," which they do literally, going about spinning a coarse yarn from a bunch of goat's hair which they hold in their hands. Their wheel is a wooden spindle, with an iron point bent like a hook, which they whirl around with considerable skill, spinning as they go.

It does not seem that human beings can exist in such a room as I have described; but hundreds do. By-and-by some of these wretched beings will be reading, in rooms where the light of God's sun can enter. But how could we urge these women in this dark filthy place to read? My heart was sick and faint, and in silent prayer we commended them to the care of our ever-pitying heavenly Father, and as quickly as we could we emerged into the pure air.

"Just step in here," said Mariam, "and see Varteeg. She will be so glad to see us, and our call will cheer her. We are at the door," and Mariam called, "Varteeg, Varteeg, open the door."

Varteeg was glad to see us, and we found her husband with her at home. He did not notice us much, but after talking for a time with the pleasant little wife, who was learning to read, even though she had four small children, we turned to him and said,

"Hohannes, are you learning to read also?"

"No," he replied; "I have no time. The rich have nothing else to do, but I have a wife and four small children to work for. How can one man do that and find time to read? Varteeg can read if she wishes, but I cannot."

"But you need the Bible as well as your wife."

"How can I learn when God has not given me the time?"

"Shall we pray, Hohannes?" I said. "Will you unite with me?"

"Oh, surely."

"But first you must understand what our prayer is to be. It is this: 'O Lord, I have so many children to care for, and have to work so hard to provide for them, that I cannot find time to read the Bible. It takes all my time to prepare this cotton for the market. Please next year to take away my children, and this cotton also, and then I shall find time to read the Bible, and learn what it teaches about my poor soul.'"

The little wheel he had been turning suddenly stopped. He was not willing to unite in such a prayer, and began to feel that he was without good excuse for not learning to read the Bible. He had felt friendly to it, and was willing his wife should learn, but for himself, he felt it would not feed his family, and that must be done.

We said a few earnest words to him, and tried to show him that the Bible would reveal One who could help him bear his daily burdens, and bring light and joy into his dark home. He was evidently moved by what we said, and when we left he rose to bid us good-by.

One more call and our day's work would be done. It was in Lizzie's school, which was on our way home. What a contrast between this cheap, rough room, and her mother's beneath it. The walls were indeed coarsely plastered, only with mud, but they were whitened with a clay wash, and the rough rafters, if unpainted, were not begrimmed with soot. The floor was of earth, but covered with coarse reed matting, and in place of the hole in the roof to let the smoke out and the light in, were windows, with oiled paper for glass.

That number of regularly-arranged pairs of little shoes at the door by which we enter, told us that twenty-five owners of small feet were there, beginning the ascent of the hill of knowledge. Wee Altom, *gold*, and her companions, Varteeg, *little rose*, Oghda, *Huldah*, Aghaveni, *dove*, and Ester, with their alphabets safely pasted upon a piece of thin board, were proud to show us that of their thirty-eight letters, they had mastered six.

The next class could read words of five syllables in the primer, while each, on a bit of slate, with a smaller piece for a pencil, wrote small words. In this land where the day's wages are from twelve to twenty cents, and that only in winter, the people cannot pay for good slates for their children. So the missionaries import the largest size, without frames, and these are cut up into pieces of different sizes. The broken bits serve for the poorest, who can have slate and pencil for a cent, or less.

Another class in this school had nearly completed their primer; the next could read in the Testament, and write with ink on paper, add columns of figures, and were studying their catechism.

The class in oral geography marched up to the map of the world, on the walls, and told us how many continents and oceans there are; and could point to the place in America from which the missionaries came.

A lesson followed in repeating Scripture, each one giving chapter and verse, and then all united in the hymn, "There is a happy land."

We closed with a short prayer, and bidding them good-by went home to supper and the evening prayer-meeting. The next day we returned to our city home.

But have we not helped you to see, dear young friends, some of the difficulties the missionary has to overcome in carrying the gospel to these poor people? Do you not think it requires great patience, wisdom, and love, to do this work? And do you not see some of the ways in which you, at home in your dear, happy native land, can help us?

One thing you can all do; you can pray that the hearts of these people may be opened to receive the Bible, that they may be inclined to learn to read it, and that their souls may be enlightened by God's Holy Spirit to understand and obey it.

CHAPTER IX.

A VISIT TO ICHMEH.

For weeks I had been planning to make a tour of the villages, which I wished very much to accomplish before the winter snows should come on. I had not once thought I could go alone, and was waiting for Susie's papa to accompany me; but his work seemed to increase rather than diminish, and I began to feel that I must start out alone. We talked over the matter and concluded it was quite safe and proper for me to go with our well-tried and faithful Garabed as an escort, especially as the distance between the villages was short, and each night I should rest at the house of some pastor or teacher—"our boys," as we called them, for they were all from our Harpoot schools.

The day was bright and propitious which had been set for the start. The black donkey was led up to the step, and I felt sure I could manage him, though once or twice he had taken the bits in his teeth, and run away, quite to my discomfort. Garabed mounted his mule, and we set out. I did not burden myself with the large bags this time. I only took my small bedstead, one quilt and a pillow, with an extra shawl, lest the cold should increase before my return. For food I put up a box of ginger snaps and some tea, determined to try the food I might get on the way. Though much of it might be unpalatable, I was not afraid of suffering with hunger, for I could come home when I pleased.

We rode on very quietly without adventure, until we arrived at a small stream, where donkey set set up his will, and would not cross. I coaxed, and Garabed used the whip, but all to no purpose; so I dismounted, and Garabed gave him a strong push, when he jumped the stream, and capered off, running some distance before Garabed could catch him. This delayed us a little, and the day was drawing to a close, when, after a six-hours' ride, which my donkey had made seven, we slowly rode up through the trees into the large village of Ichmeh, and alighted at the house of good pastor Krekore, where I well knew I should be a welcome guest. He was at the door before we were, and helped me into his nice new house, the best in the village.

This pastor is the "Little Gregory" mentioned in Grace Illustrated, where his house is called a "mouse-hole," but he had since moved into a new one with four nice rooms. The parlor was not yet furnished, but as he waited patiently for the house, he will doubtless in due time have all the rooms nicely fitted up. This house was built for the pastor by a very energetic man in the village, who has a large family to provide for, but who loves the pastor very much, and not only meant, when he began the work, that he should have the house, but intended to fit up the parlor, or guest-room, in good oriental style; that is, not with chairs, tables, mirrors and pictures, as we should, but with carpets and cushions. But the house cost more than he anticipated, and times were hard, so he said, "We must wait for a season for the rest." The four rooms are built around an open hall in the centre, which makes it very pleasant in summer.

Protestantism has done much to improve this village of Ichmeh. One of the best houses belongs to three brothers, two of whom are professed Protestants, and the other more than half persuaded. These brothers are all of marked ability, and when the gospel came to them, they could not stay in their dark, dirty home. Two of them came out boldly from their nominal Christianity, the other believed in heart, but hoped to have all the benefits of the gospel while remaining in the church in which he had been born.

There was a priest in this village also who became a Protestant. His name was Emmanuel. He could not withstand the desire to read the Bible, so he bought one secretly, and took it to his home. After the children were asleep for the night, he told his wife what he had done, and bringing the book out of its hiding-place, he read till a late hour, while Marta, his wife, listened. This they continued to do till the third night, when they both wept over it. The priest, looking towards his wife, said solemnly, "Wife, if this is true, we are lost."

"If this is true let us receive it," she replied.

"What, become Protestants?"

"Yes," said the heroic wife.

"We shall have to beg from house to house, wife, if we do."

"Let us go, then. I will take your hand and go with you. Our souls are of more importance than our bodies."

The next morning they went to the service in the Protestant chapel, and told Pastor Krekore and the brethren what they had resolved to do. It made a great stir in the village, for it was at once

A VISIT TO ICHMEH. 97

noised from one end of the place to the other, and people ran to the church and marketplace to find out about it. They had another priest, an old, gray-headed man. He was much excited. He sent some of the men to talk with "this insane man," as he called him, and to persuade him to repent of his wickedness and folly; and when he found it availed nothing, a curse was pronounced upon the heretic. They went to his house, and threatened to pull it down over his head. They declared he should starve, threw mud and stones at the house, and said that God would curse him and his family. When Marta went out to the fountain for water, the women would scream at her from their housetops, "Prote! prote! You are worse than a Turk. We put you up on twelve cushions the night your husband was made priest, and now we will pull you down again. You are no longer priestess, but a prode" (leper).

Of course this was all very hard for her to bear, but she told me when I called upon in her humble home, that the dear Saviour, whom she had learned about in the Bible, and who had opened their eyes, helped them to bear all this persecution.

When we arrived at the pastor's house, Marta, his wife, was not at home. She had gone to a neighbor's to have some washing done. Formerly the women carried their washing to the fountain in the centre of the village, but I think it cost some of them a great deal of suffering. Many of them were crippled with rheumatism and neuralgia, which was doubtless caused by their standing in the water while washing, as they were obliged to do. Now they have adopted the custom of doing the washing at their houses. Two or three families join together and have what we should call a washing-bee. The pastor's wife was away for this purpose. He set off immediately to call her, and she quickly came, and on her return prepared the evening meal of cracked wheat. The little table, as I explained before, or what we should call a tray, was placed on a low stool, the wheat, seasoned with a little meat, was served in a deep dish and placed in the centre, while thin cakes of bread were laid upon the outside, and a copper-dish of buttermilk was placed beside the wheat. Garabed brought us a cup of tea, and some of the ginger-snaps we had brought; wooden spoons were given to each, the blessing was asked, and we began our dinner.

Their dinner was always a very simple repast. Once, as a special honor to me, they had a chicken soup, and after that was served, a *pilav*—cooked rice with butter—and the chicken from which the soup was made. The people are very frugal, and we sometimes think they do not eat enough to make them strong. They have but few luxuries, but some of them have more than Joseph and Mary probably had in their humble home in Nazareth; and when Jesus went out from that home to be a preacher, he doubtless often satisfied his hunger on a very simple meal. We read of the barley-loaves and of the broiled fish which he prepared on the shore of Galilee. "Little Gregory," this good pastor of Ichmeh, had few worldly goods and no luxuries, but it seemed to me his house was like the home in Bethany where the Master loved to go and rest.

Pastor Krekore gave me his little study for the night. He and Garabed put up my bedstead, and then he borrowed a bed, and with my quilt I slept very nicely till the village cocks told me it was time to make preparation for breakfast.

Our breakfast consisted of fried eggs and bread. Then the pastor had family devotions, after which he invited me to go with him to a village about two miles away. Hohannes, a very earnest helper, was laboring there, and had urged pastor Krekore to bring me to his village. He hoped I would be able to help him by persuading some of the women there to read. I was glad to go with him, for I felt he would be an assistance in this work.

The donkey was made ready, the pastor took Garabed's mule, and we started out on our second day's visit.

CHAPTER X.

ACROSS THE EUPHRATES.

THE day was cold, but I buttoned my fur-lined sacque snugly about me, and rode comfortably along over mountain and hillside till we came to a branch of the Euphrates. Across this stream lay the pleasant village of Oozoonova (Long Meadow) to which we were going.

We had to wait till the ugly-looking scow should come over to take us to the other side. Here again we had a most comical scene with my independent little donkey; but he was at length conquered, and we all arrived in safety on the opposite bank, and after a short ride we dismounted in front of Hohannes' quarters.

Hohannes had no wife; he was still a student at Harpoot, and spent only his winter vacations in this place. He had commenced his work here under great discouragements. When he first came to this village there was but one Protestant in it, but now he has a congregation of fifty men and twelve women.

The day he came to Oozoonova he entered his little room, where there was scarcely space enough for himself and the box that contained his clothes and books, and with a trembling heart he took out his Bible, read a few of its sweet promises, and then kneeling down, commended himself to Him who alone could help him in such a hard place.

He then went to the chapel, lighted a fire, and taking his board and wooden mallets, went to the roof. This board, called a *gochnag*, is used as a bell to call the people to morning and evening prayers. The Armenians were accustomed to send the sexton from house to house for this purpose. The board gong was an invention of one of the early missionaries, and became so popular that it was adopted all over the plain of Harpoot by the Armenian Christians as well as the Protestants.

Hohannes found a good place, and hanging the board by the strings attached to each end, struck it vigorously to call the people to the evening service. Two persons came; one, the Protestant we mentioned before, and the other a spy sent in by those who hated the Protestants, to report all who might be present. On subsequent days more came in, the audience increasing one by one, till the little chapel was filled, and they opened a larger one, and set aside one part of this for the women. Only one woman came for a long time, till an earnest sister from Harpoot, on her way to another place, spent a night here, and invited her hostess to go with her to the evening service in the chapel. She consented, and was greatly pleased with Hohannes' simple, earnest words about Jesus. "Why, I can understand all he says," said she. "How unlike our priests!" The priests read in ancient Armenian, and though in talking they use the modern, it is only a low, confused sound, which scarcely reaches the poor women behind the lattice-work in the gallery.

At the time of my visit the number of women had increased to twelve; but Hohannes was not satisfied to have them only come to church. He earnestly desired that they should learn to read, and it was for the advancement of this object that he had anticipated my visit. He met me, however, on that cold morning with a sad face.

"Hanum," said he, "you have come at a very unfortunate time. I wish you to see the sisters, but they will not come here," (he had no wife,) "and I am afraid to take you to their houses to-day. We have had a three-days' feast after a wedding, and the people are well drunken, excepting the Protestants and the younger brides. They would not use any violence against you, but they may say unbecoming words, and I should feel it as much as if they said it to my mother. But, hanum, I do wish you to see the sisters; I have so longed to have you come."

I was not afraid, however, and desired to start immediately, and Hohannes agreed to go with me. We went first to the house of a large family near where there were six women. Some of the young men came to the chapel, but none of the women. They were all convinced, however of the truth of our teachings. The youngest had learned to read in another village, and the others desired to, and their husbands would consent, if the mother-in-law and the oldest brother could be persuaded to allow it.

We went in, Pastor Krekore following. Hohannes introduced me to Elmas, the eldest of the women, as the mother-in-law was away. She received me very politely, and invited me to sit down, placing a new large cushion for me. The house was neat, even to the mud floor, which was almost as hard as cement, and it was very evident that these were the rich people of the village, one of the "first families." Several of the younger brides were dressed in silk, with a profusion of silver jewelry about them. They had all been at the wedding, as it was at the house of a relative.

Hohannes brought a large Bible, one of five he had sold in the village. I felt quite at ease when he said, "The hanum will read this to you." The women gathered close about me, and I read to them a part of the Sermon on the Mount, pausing at intervals to explain. They were much interested in all I read and said to them, and were quite free to talk to me, even though several of the young men had come near, and Hohannes also. They seemed greatly pleased that he had kept his promise to bring me to them. The oldest, Elmas, said, "We wish to read, but our mother-in-law will not let us. She says it will make us lazy and impudent." Their mouths were tied up with a black cloth, as is the custom with the city brides; but as they talked, they threw back their veils, and pulled the black cloth down under the chin, and were very bright and chatty. Soon I saw a sudden movement. Their faces were all covered in a moment, and they rose to their feet.

Looking toward the door I saw a man, about thirty years of age, enter. I concluded he was the patriarch, or head of the house, and I also arose. Hohannes introduced him as the eldest brother, and I invited him him to sit on the cushion above me, as the most honorable place.

He declined, saying, "I am not fit to sit beside you. I have been drinking wine."

I replied, "I will excuse you, brother, if you will drink no more."

I had won him. He sat down beside me, and when he noticed the Bible, asked me to read on.

I said, "I have been reading to the women; it will be more proper for Pastor Krekore to read to you," and I rose and handed the Bible to the pastor; but he insisted that I should read, and the pastor returned me the Bible, saying he would prefer to have me. I read to him the Saviour's prayer in John 17th. He was much interested, and said, "It is a good thing to read the Bible, but we are ignorant, and our priests know nothing."

"I am glad you have a Bible in your house, brother," I said. "I hope you read it daily and will let the brides read also. They too have souls. The Bible is God's letter, sent down from heaven to teach us the way of salvation. What good will it do if we put it in a box, and never take it out to find out what it says? I think if you will consent, the brides will all gladly learn to read."

"Let them read if they wish," he replied, "but let them not speak to me or uncover their faces."

Here his mother came in, and we arose to receive her, while he kept his seat. She sat down on the other side of me, when he said, "Mother, the hanum wishes these brides to read. What do you say?"

"They have no time," she answered politely; "we have to work for our living. Reading is a good thing, but makes brides lazy and disobedient."

"I have to work," I said, "and can do more from the very fact that I read; the Bible helps me. It makes people more obedient, and shows us that it is wrong to be lazy. We need food for our bodies, and we must labor for this, but the Bible tells us how to get food for our hungry, starving souls. God has given you these brides to care for, and will you keep them all the time at work for these bodies that will die by-and-by? What will you answer to the Lord when he asks you about their souls? He has given us time to care for body and soul too, and he will help us if we ask him."

"Will he help us spin, weave, cook and sew?"

"Yes, he has said so, but he says, 'Seek *first* the kingdom of God and his righteousness, and all these things shall be added unto you.'"

"Well," said she, "then they may read, if they will do their work, and not trouble me."

Hohannes was much pleased at the result of our conversation, and has a strong hope that this whole family before long will become Christians.

CHAPTER XI.

AT THE FEAST.

WHILE I was talking with this man and his mother an invitation came for us to go to the house of feasting, and Hohannes thought it best to accept it, as one of the brothers in that house was the most influential Protestant in the village, and a true Christian. He said I should see more women there than if I went from house to house; and as it was the hour when most of the men would be at the market-place, the opportunity to see the women would be still more favorable. The feast, according to the usual custom, was given in the house of the bridegroom's godfather on the third day after the marriage.

The old lady with whom I had just been talking offered to go with me, and Hohannes and Krekore went on before to make sure that all was right.

Kevork, the Protestant brother, met us at the door and invited us in. I wished to go to the part of the room where the women were gathered, but he would not listen for a moment to such an arrangement. I must have the first place in his house, and he would bring the women to that part of the room.

His wife and several others came and gave me the usual salutations, though they seemed to feel out of place. Altoon, the youngest brother's wife, sat down near me, and Hohannes said to me aside, "If you can persuade that woman to read, the whole village will follow. She has no children, is very bright, and will learn quickly."

"My husband will not let me read," said Altoon.

"He will not hinder you," replied Hohannes, "and Kevork says he will get you a primer, and when you finish that, a Testament."

"Let Shushan, his wife, learn first," said she, "and then I will think about it."

The truth was she was unwilling to be the leader—ashamed to be called the reformer of her village. The women of our happy America can scarcely realize how much it costs the poor, ignorant daughters of Armenia to read. Many a Christian woman at home would be unwilling even to repeat a verse of Scripture in a prayer-meeting, simply because it is against the custom; and can they wonder if these poor creatures are held in the same iron grip of custom. For my own part I am amazed that so many do break away from its tyranny, and learn. I often think they manifest more persistent earnestness than would be found among our own more highly-favored sisters. They have everything to drag them down. If we had been brought up in such dark, dirty, cold homes, we should soon be as degraded as they.

The gospel is producing great changes there, but when will these homes all be changed? Oh, that is the question so often asked. It was put to me by one of our Armenian pastors not long since. It seemed to him he could not wait for his people to be elevated by the slow means we were employing. Sometimes he was very sad and dejected over the condition of his people. But I told him how long it took to bring our country up to where it now is. I showed him a picture of the first church built by our Pilgrim fathers not far from Plymouth Rock, and he saw that his own church was a much better building.

"We must go on patiently laboring," I said, "and all the blessings you are longing for will come."

"But, hanum, I wish to see it in my lifetime! A few years hence I shall be in my grave."

I wish all the people in America enjoying homes made beautiful by the light and knowledge of the Saviour, could have seen this young man as we talked together, handsome and manly, his brilliant black eyes saddened by a longing that could not be satisfied. I am sure it would stimulate them to do more for this benighted land.

But we must go back to the home in Oozoonova, where we had been invited to the feast. The copper table had been brought in, and the feast was ready.

"Please be seated here, hanum," said Kevork.

I politely thanked him; but seeing the women around the table in an opposite quarter of the room, I moved in that direction, saying that I preferred to observe their custom, and would eat with the women. He seemed shocked at the idea, and Pastor Krekore and Hohannes both protested. He then called his wife and the other women to come and sit by me. But they did not come. They said they had taken dinner and were not hungry, but the true reason was that they thought it unwomanly to eat with the men. They said to me, "It is your custom." And then they asked, "Why are these women honored so much more than we are?

Why even our own husbands honor them! We will read, and then we too shall have a place as equals with our husbands."

So this helped our influence with the women more than anything else could have done. This was the first time a missionary lady had been to that village; and the result was that several of these women began at once to read, and when I go back I expect to find that most of the sisters in Oozoonova are reading.

Kevork placed a high cushion for me at the table, and after the blessing they gave me a spoon, and I dipped with them into the several dishes. There was the buttermilk soup, which is a common and quite aristocratic dish among them, and I bravely ate some of it; then gladly seized an opportunity to put my spoon into the next dish, which tasted as nice as oyster soup. Several kinds of meats were served, and Kevork was much gratified to have me like them, as I certainly did. The food was all well cooked, and the bread was sweet and light, though not very white. I enjoyed the nice fresh butter, adding a little salt; also the honey, and the cheese from the Koordish mountains, which seemed quite like that of home manufacture.

After the meats came fruits. They know nothing of pies and puddings in Armenia. We sometimes find rice cooked in milk, with sugar or honey on it, and a kind of sweet paste, but these are rare. But grapes, apples, pears, apricots, and melons abound, with a great variety of nuts. These, with bastic, a kind of dried paste, and candy, are sometimes used in the cities as dessert, but not often in the villages.

After our meal was finished, the washbowl and ewer were brought to each one, a young girl following with a towel. The washbowl was of copper, with a cover filled with holes, and a cake of soap on a little plate on the central part of the cover. The ewer was a very pretty copper-vessel. One towel served for all.

The table removed, Kevork brought the Bible, and Pastor Krekore read and prayed, when we mounted our animals and hastened to the river, fearing it would be too late to cross that night. We reached the shore just in time for the last crossing, and were soon climbing up the steep side of a mountain. It was dark when we rode into the village of Shukhaji, where we spent the second night, at the house of the earnest preacher, Menzo, and his nice little wife Mariam.

The gospel has done much for this family. It

has lifted them out of poverty and ignorance, and made them intelligent, earnest Christians. The mother with a large family to care for, found time to work among the women after Varteeg, the Bible-woman, had left, inviting them to the parsonage, where she or her daughter Sara would give them a lesson.

Varteeg, whose name signifies *Little Rose*, was a native of this village. She had graduated at our seminary, and then returned, and for several years was Bible-woman and teacher. She afterwards married a native helper, and went with him to another village, where they were doing great good. Her loss was deeply felt in this place, and Mariam, the pastor's wife, sought earnestly to supply her place. Though often confined to her bed with painful sickness, she would never send the women away who came to her. She would take the baby from the oldest girl, Sara, and bid her give the lesson, which she would herself explain while bolstered up with pillows. Sara could not have been more than ten years old at that time. She came to the seminary at Harpoot, two years after, and from that time always taught in Shukhaji during the vacations.

CHAPTER XII.

GULASER'S HOUSEHOLD

OUR route the next morning lay along the side of a spur of the Taurus mountains, whose snow-capped peaks on our left touched the fleecy clouds, while on our right, at their base, not more than two miles away, flowed the Euphrates, its banks green with fields of springing grain; the two opposing seasons a fit emblem of the hand-to-hand conflict going on between the two moral forces in this immediate region.

We reached Ichmeh after an hour's ride, and found the pastor's wife and Garabed quite anxious about us. As they had expected us the evening before, Garabed had prepared a hot soup, thinking we should be tired and hungry after our day's work, not once imagining we were at that hour feasting at the house of Kevork. When we reached the pastor's house, we found we had been invited to breakfast at Gulaser's.

And now, as Susie asks, "Who is Gulaser?" I doubt not all our readers will be gratified to know something of his history. He was the man who had been so much interested in building Pastor Krekore's house, and was one of the most prosperous and influential men in Ichmeh.

About thirty years ago, when a bright young lad, he was betrothed to a handsome girl in a village, about eight hours' ride distant. Both belonged to the higher class of society, and of course jewelry and other gifts were liberally exchanged, though custom forbade that they should see each other. In the course of time preparations for a great wedding began at the house of Boghos, the silversmith, the brother of Gulaser. The invitations were sent out; not cards, as we send, but an apple, a pear, or a quince, to each invited guest. The women in their long white veils, or wimples, were going and coming at the silversmith's. Soon the tailor was seen entering the house with a large bundle, and the women by this understood that the bridal-dress was ready. It is etiquette in that land for the bridegroom to prepare the wedding-dress for the bride, and the tailor makes it, as they have no dressmakers, the women knowing very little about sewing. The dress required very little fitting. It was like a long sack, and if the bride was very young, as is usually the case, it was taken up under the girdle in front, and allowed to trail behind. It was made large enough for her when she should be an old woman. The sleeves were loose and open, faced with silk, sometimes yellow, sometimes scarlet, and hung from the wrists from half to three-quarters of a yard in length. Over this garment was worn a richly-embroidered jacket of velvet or broadcloth. It was embroidered with gold cord, which did not tarnish with wear, was quite expensive, and very handsome. The bridal-dress was usually of silk; sometimes of the richest Turk-satin, scarlet, yellow, green, or purple. Even the poorest must have silk of some quality, though the money must be saved from other seemingly needful expenses.

The bride's mother prepares the trousseau, with the exception of the bridal dress, and begins often when her daughter is a mere babe, that the chest may be well filled. Everything is thought of which she can need for her person or house, even to a tiny pair of tongs to hold a coal of fire for her husband and his male friends to light their pipes or cigarettes. The number of articles of course is determined by the wealth of the parties.

When the bridegroom's friends go to bring the bride, they take the wedding garments. These must first, however, be blessed by the priest. He is called in for this purpose, and after the consecration the garments are folded with great care, and a large handkerchief, often embroidered, or made of bright pieces of silk or calico, is folded over them and fastened with a silver button or pin. When they arrive, the bride is dressed in the presence of her friends who have come to prepare her for her departure.

In this case the bride had to go a day's journey. Boghos, Gulaser's eldest brother, with both male and female friends, went to bring her. A feast was given to the party at the bride's house, which continued late into the night; and the next morning they started at an early hour, hurrying on the weeping girl, and leaving behind the wailing crowd of women who had gathered to say good-by. Several of her near relatives, brothers or cousins, accompanied her till she reached the house of the bridegroom's relatives, but they do not enter, as they there leave her to her new friends. The wedding at the bridegroom's house is a day of rejoicing, for they gain a daughter; but the bride's friends are expected to be desolate, for they lose one, and it would be improper for them to be found enjoying the festivities.

Late in the afternoon the sound of drum, fife,

and violin, was heard at the entering in of Ichmeh, and the cry went round, "The bride is coming." By the time the party had reached the trees at the foot of the hill, a large number of men and women on horses, and a crowd of children of every class, had joined them. Gulaser was not among the number, though you may be sure he had been watching the cavalcade ever since his keen vision had descried it far away.

According to custom the bride could not come to his home, but stopped over night with friends. In the morning the happy bridegroom, mounted on a fine horse, a man beside him leading another, and escorted by numerous relatives and companions, went to the house and took her to the church where the marriage ceremony was performed. Then with music and dancing he took her to his home.

Gulaser had no mother living, so the wife of Boghos, the eldest brother, received the bride and led her to one corner of the room, where she stood the whole evening, closely veiled. The third day this veil was removed and her mouth bound up with a black cloth, and the veil, usually worn by the women, thrown over her head and face, coming down to her shoulders.

This young bride of thirty years ago was the

hostess who received us that morning at Gulaser's house. Her name is Hach-hatoon, or *Lady-cross*. She had become a dignified, handsome matron, worthy of all the honor she received in this household of fifty souls. Her children and grandchildren were now about her, and she seemed a real queen among them.

She had learned to read. Some time before this, her son Marderose, who had been to hear the Protestant preacher, brought home a primer, and urged his mother to take lessons.

"I have a large family to care for," she said, "and I cannot find time."

Marderose replied, "You must, mother; we will help you," referring to his younger brothers, who had also learned.

They united their entreaties with his, and gave the mother no chance for excuse. They would bring the primer and hold it before her till she had actually learned the letters, and then her own interest was so awakened that she needed but little aid. She had such a desire to learn that she kept the book beside her, whatever she was doing, and hurried through her work that she might gain time for study. She kept it under her cushion when she was making bread at their baking-bees, where they are accustomed to bake bread enough for a month; and when she got ahead a little in the process, would pull it out and spell bread, or some other word. She was greatly pleased when she could make out a word.

I shall never forget how she looked the first time I saw her in church with her hymn-book in her hand. She did not go for a long time to the Protestant church, though her husband and sons attended regularly. She went still to the old church with the wife of Boghos, who was quite an invalid, and had for years given the control of the house into Hackhatoon's care.

Her sons were delighted with Krekore, who was then only a preacher in the village. They would tell her of his sweet words, and won her before she was conscious of it. She wanted to go to hear him, but there was Boghos; would he not be angry? He had said he would beat his own wife if she dared to go near "those Protes." Boghos had always been kind to her, Gulaser's wife, and she did not like to displease him. His shop was on the street by which she must go to the chapel, and he would surely know if she went.

But she did not give up the thought of going, and one day she crept along under the wall in front of Boghos' shop, and entered the chapel. She was deeply interested in the earnest words of the preacher, and "from that time," said she, "I could not stay away." Boghos, if he knew of her going, said nothing about it, and his wife finally overcame her fears, and went with Hach-hatoon to an evening service. When she opened the chapel-door to come home, she met her husband face to face. In telling the story afterwards, she said, "I trembled all over. I knew I deserved a beating for my disobedience, and believed I should get it. But when he came home, he took my hands, looked at me, and said, 'Yeghesa, did I not tell you I would beat you if you ever dared go to that place?' Then he dropped my hands and pleasantly said, 'I wont beat you, Yeghesa.' He too had been listening to Krekore's preaching, and was convinced of its truth." The four, Boghos and Gulaser with their wives, are now members of the Ichmeh church, together with many others of this patriarchal family. Marderose, the son, is one of the deacons.

The history of this family is a beautiful illustration of the words of Jesus. "The kingdom of heaven is like leaven that a woman took and hid in three measures of meal, till the whole was leavened." Only it was some little boys who took the leaven, in this instance, and hid it in their mother's heart. They heard the truth, and loving their mother dearly, they wanted her to know about the precious treasure they had found. They won her first by their affectionate earnestness, and when the truth entered her heart, it made her so much more lovely that others about her were won, and thus it spread in the family until the rest of the adults were reached by it.

Some of the members of this household would be ornaments in any church. There is a Young Men's Christian Association in Ichmeh, which is composed largely of the young men of this extremely interesting family. When the missionaries go to Ichmeh, the house of Boghos and Gulaser is always open to receive them, and the good women there are ever ready to minister to their wants. God has blessed them too in their basket and store, for these people are prospering in business, and are loved and honored by all who know them. It is an honorable mention of one, when introduced, to have it said, " This person is from the Gulaser house."

By this story I have told you, dear young friends, you see how much you are doing, when by your efforts at home you are raising the money to pay for teachers, preachers, and books, and by these means are hiding the leaven of truth in these far-off and benighted lands. And the boys and girls in America may learn from this story of little Marderose and his brothers, what they can do in their own homes and neighborhoods, if they have the love of Jesus in their hearts.

But by this time you will be ready to hear something of our visit.

At eight o'clock they sent for us, and when we reached the house we were seated by the *kusa*, a frame like a low table, with a thick rug thrown over it. A pot of coals was placed under the frame, which was lined with tin. This was their heating apparatus. We sat on the cushions near the wall, with cushions at our backs, and were invited to put our feet under the frame, as you would under a table, and the rug was thrown over them. We were soon very comfortable; it was like sitting over a register.

The food was served on the usual copper table on the top of the kusa; and was the nicest repast I ever had enjoyed in that region. But I will not stop to describe it, as I have spent so much time in telling you about the family. Breakfast being over, the table was removed by the younger members of the household, who were in attendance. The older women then came in, and all sat down, while Hachhatoon brought the Bible, and several hymn-books. Pastor Krekore was invited to read, and lead in prayer, and we all sung. It was a pleasant service, and when it was concluded we continued to sing until the time for the midday female prayer-meeting, and I went with the women to the chapel, where nearly a hundred of the sisters had gathered at the sound of the wooden bell. Some doubtless came on that occasion because they knew that I would be there, but this meeting is generally well attended. Marta, the pastor's wife, being an invalid cannot conduct it, and sometimes the pastor takes charge, but usually it is left in the care of Hackhatoon, and her husband's sister Loosig, who is also a faithful worker in the village. Markareed, also, who was now confined to her home with a lame foot, has taken an important part in the work among the women of Ichmeh.

Most of the women had their hymn-books ready to open to the hymn, and what is better, they all joined in the singing. Every head was bowed at the opening prayer, and one could hardly help feeling it to be a privilege to unite with such worshippers at a throne of grace.

Mariam, the Bible-woman, read the story of the Prodigal Son, and asked me to explain it. We talked about it for a few minutes, and then one after another led in prayer, asking blessings for themselves, and that the kind Heavenly Father would bring back every wandering child. Their prayers are earnest and simple. They go to God as the little child goes to its mother, when hungry, and asks for something to eat. I have often felt that they were more acceptable than mine, and I could tell you many cases where answers to their requests seemed very direct. Sometimes we, who have been their teachers, sit at their feet as learners.

At the close of the prayer-meeting the animals were brought, and we started for the village of Haboosic.

CHAPTER XIII.

THE TOUR CONTINUED AND ENDED.

THE earnest pastor Garabed and his wife Badashan were training their church in Haboosie to be one of the most spiritual in our field. We enjoyed the evening service in the large and well-filled chapel, and the women's prayer-meeting the next morning, at which a good number of the sisters were present.

They were very glad to see me, and wished we could visit them oftener. I reminded them of the hundreds of villages we had to visit, and of the work we had to do in the city in educating the teachers and preachers needed for all. We had given them good pastor Garabed and his wife, who were doing better for them than we could.

I was glad to find them making so much effort to read the Bible. One woman with a sour face said. "You at the city have nothing to do; you can read all you wish;" but a pleasant faced sister instantly exclaimed, in a reproving tone, "Soos!" (Silence!) "do you not know that these hanums do a great deal more work than we do?"

After the early prayer-meeting I asked Badashan when we could call on the women. "As soon as the smoke rises," she replied. And certainly it was desirable that their close, dingy rooms should be cleared of smoke before we attempted to visit them.

We went to the most distant part of the village first that we might gain time. We found the women all loved the pastor, and his wife, and it was evident that Badashan was a true helpmate to her husband. They gave her a position above them, and she used this position for their good. She was their Bible-woman, their leader in the prayer-meetings, and in their homes, for she was a model housekeeper. Garabed was earnest, but very dignified, seldom forgetting his cane when he went abroad; and his people were pleased with this. But Badashan would take her clean baby on her arm, and a bowl of soup in her hand, and go to some sick neighbor with her bright face all radiant with smiles. In her eagerness to make somebody happy she seemed to forget that she was the pastoress. She had a sunny face, and wherever she went scattered pearls, which no one thought of trampling, but only of gathering as precious treasure.

"Here, is a house you must visit, hanum," she

said. "It is the home of Deacon Hagop, but one of the women here is very bitter. She is always talking against the Protestants, and does much harm, as she is a talented woman."

We went in through a long, dark entrance. It seemed to me very long. Not a ray of light pierced the gloom, and the floor was so uneven that I feared to fall at every step. But Badashan knew the way, and gave me her hand to guide me. When we reached the family-room, we found it large, and very neat for a village-room. The smoke was still clinging to the corners, and in the top of the apartment, but did not trouble us. A large, resolute-looking woman arose, and gave us the usual salutations, and invited us to sit by the fireplace. We were cold, for it was late in November, and the mountains about us were white with snow. She uncovered the hole in the floor and said, "Put your feet inside, hanum." I obeyed, more to please her than myself, for it seemed like putting my feet into a hot well. The hot air was fragrant with the food cooking inside, which reminded me that Esau's savory dish for his blind father was probably cooked in much the same way.

By the time I was thoroughly warm, all the brides of the household of forty souls, had gathered around, and given us the salutations, but none of them sat down, except the one who first received us, who was evidently the wife of the patriarch of this Oriental home.

"I presume you all know how to read, as this is the house of Deacon Hagop," I said.

This was just the question my hostess was waiting for. It gave her an opportunity to say just what she thought of the "Protes," and with sarcastic vehemence she piled abuse on abuse, till she had exhausted herself and the language.

I then quietly remarked, "Sister, I wish you would become a Protestant, and teach us how to live."

This was very unexpected to her. She thought I would defend the Protestants; and then she would have a chance for argument. She threw up her arms, leaned back against the wall, and laughed heartily, exclaiming, "You are a strange woman, hanum! I never saw such a Prote before." Then, calling to the other women, she said, "Bring out the table; this woman must have some breakfast."

A little wooden table, almost as black as the smoky walls, was forthwith brought, and placed near me, and nice fresh bread, butter and honey, with some milk, dried cream and cheese, were placed upon it. Then she went to the fire-hole, and took out a covered earthen pot, from which, with a wooden ladle, she dipped out a large copper dish full of soup, and placing it in the centre of the table, invited us to begin.

"But shall we not have a blessing?"

"Certainly."

I motioned to Badashan, and she, with much fervor, asked the Divine blessing.

Wooden spoons were handed us, and we all began to dip into the centre dish, which sent forth the same appetizing odor that greeted me while I was warming my feet. I was so impolite as to ask what this nice soup was made of, and the lady, seemingly complimented by my question, replied that it was made of little watermelons. It was equal to the best French vegetable soup I ever tasted, and I enjoyed it highly. I was very hungry, as I had gone nine hours without eating, and made a good breakfast, or dinner, as I might as well call it. Our hostess seemed greatly pleased to see me eat so heartily, and to have me praise her food, and turning to me, she said laughingly, "You like our food, and do not defend the Protes."

"We hold up Christ as a pattern, not the Prottestants," I replied. "He only is the perfect example, and it is always safe to follow him. The Protestants are imperfect, because they fail in likeness to Christ. It will do you no good to look at them, sister. Read the Bible for yourself, and live as Christ wishes you to, and then you will pity those Protestants who seem so imperfect to you. God has given you a bright mind; what will you say when he calls you to give an account? Is it wise to starve your soul, by feeding it on the husks of other people's faults?"

I felt that I had won that woman to my side, that is, she became my friend, but she did not accept Christ. She listened while we read and prayed, and was much softened, but I have not yet learned of her becoming a true Christian. She had a very proud heart that kept her from yielding to the Saviour. And though she could not read, she had a pride of intellect, as I might express it, or a feeling of superiority over her neighbors in the village, which was a still greater obstacle. But I still hope to hear that she has found her perfect ideal in Christ, and, accepting him, has become all she thinks others ought to be. I shall never cease to be interested in her, and in the thousands of Armenia's daughters, who, if blest with a Christian education, would fill the highest positions of womanhood with dignity and grace.

An hour's ride from Haboosie, the next day, brought us to the little village of Aghansi, where the preacher Hagop, and Eva, his neat sensible wife, were laying the foundations of a Christian civilization, in a very quiet but effectual manner.

There was little to encourage them when they began in this dark, rude village. Not a house could be found really fit to live in. Yet these good people joyfully settled themselves in the room provided, which was to be chapel, schoolhouse and dwelling. The villagers looked up to them as a higher class of beings, and came in from curiosity to see them, and hear them read and talk about the new Bible they had brought. Their neatness, their intelligence, and their piety won the people. They saw and felt the contrast between the home of Hagop and Eva and their own; yet they knew that the preacher and his wife were not foreigners like the missionaries, but were villagers like themselves. Whence then the difference? Ah, they had been at the schools in Harpoot, and had there learned all these new things.

It was of little use for the priest to curse those who went to hear these "Protes;" for they would go. Among them was a carpenter, who, when he had heard, gladly received the truth into his heart, and acted it out in his life.

"We must have a larger room for our chapel," said he, "and our preacher and his wife cannot see in that hole of a place. We must do something." He knew that the Protestants in the village were few and poor, but with the promise of a little help he went to work.

The villagers had no money to give, but they promised work. They could make the brick, sift the dirt, and help in other ways. The missionaries supplied a little needed money. The carpenter worked every spare moment, often going in the night to another village to bring lumber, because he wanted all the daylight for building.

At the time I was there the chapel was so far finished that they could worship in it; and Hagop and Eva were living in the prophet's chamber on its side. The carpenter had put up this room for them, and a small kitchen, perhaps ten feet square, next to it. It was to this dwelling that we went when we came into the village at this time. We had no trouble in finding it, as it was the only new house in the place.

Hagop saw us coming, and came to meet us.

I followed him up the ladder-like steps, and found Eva standing in the door to greet me. She looked pretty in her neat, but patched dress, her hair nicely braided, and a small black handkerchief tied gracefully over her head. Her face was all smiles as she led me into her little home—the only *home*, I might say, in the village.

Let me give you my impressions by telling you what Hohannes, a young man of the village, said about it. He came in to see us in the evening. He sat near the door, and after I had ceased talking with him, he leaned his face upon his hands and gazed about the room. I knew from his looks he was drinking in its beauties; so I said, "Hohannes, this seems to you a very nice place, does it not?"

"O hanum, it is like a palace to me; I love to come here!"

I wish every person, young or old, who has had a share in the missionary work, could have seen him as he said these words, and then could have looked with us about the room.

The walls were plastered with *clean* mud. At one end was the window, three feet by four, with one small pane of glass in the centre, to look through, the rest filled with oiled paper, to let in the light and keep out the cold. Opposite the window was the door. At the right, as we entered, hung a rude bookcase, filled with books, at each side a small picture, and under the bookcase a calico-case for thread and thimble, made by some little girl in America, and given to Eva by a missionary lady, while she was at school at Harpoot. The mud-floor was covered with coarse matting made of reeds, with some pieces of Koordish carpeting spread at the sides to sit upon. There was one cushion in the corner, at the right of the window, and I was invited to sit on that, while Eva brought another for my back. The bedding, nicely folded and covered with a coarse cloth, was piled in another corner, and the cushion for my back came from that. This was the palace-home that thrilled the heart of Hohannes, and covered the face of Eva with smiles. And it was a real home, such as we are trying to plant all over the plains of Armenia, and to the very tops of old Taurus.

How I wish that thousands who live in real palaces, and travel in palace-cars, could once visit this, and then the home of the carpenter who built it, with its black sides, the cattle separated from the sittingroom by only a low wall, and hear him, when he said to the missionary, "Would that it were not necessary to take this money; but I have done all I could, badvellie." I think they would feel as I did, that this poor carpenter resembled his Master, the carpenter of Nazareth, and perhaps will have a higher position in the palace of the King of kings, than some of us who dwell in ceiled houses and have many luxuries.

Woman's share in the work to be done in these villages was evident here. Hagop preached the gospel, but Eva and her well-kept home were needed to illustrate and enforce it.

The room was too small for me to put up my bedstead, and leave others room to lie down. So Garabed took my shawl and with Hagop's help, soon separated space enough for me, and spread my quilt upon the reed carpet. Eva tucked me nicely in, and although the bed was hard I was soon asleep.

The next morning Eva had a chicken nicely cooked for breakfast, and we were soon after on our way to Harpoot after a tour of nine days. We were six hours on the road, and the piercing north wind chilled me through before I reached home. Garabed was very thoughtful, alighting several times to put extra wraps around me, but it is not easy to keep warm on horseback, facing a cold wind.

"O mamma," exclaimed Susie, "how well I remember the day you came home. It was so cold that the plants all froze the night before, and in the morning papa came in and said, 'Mamma will be very cold; Mariam, you must keep a good fire in the stove.'"

Yes, and I remember well how Susie and all the rest of the dear ones looked when I arrived. It seemed as though I had been gone nineteen instead of nine days, and when I entered our cheerful sittingroom, I thought of Hohannes, and wondered what he would say if he could see that. Before I had taken off my wraps, a villager came in, and papa told him that I had been away on a tour to the villages. He looked at me with wonder, and said, "Hanum, how can you go to our dirty homes? Your home is so light and beautiful, and ours are dark and filthy. We wonder that you ever go to the villages; surely it is not to please yourselves. Your religion must be different from ours." He reminded me of a woman from Karungerd, who once came to our house. When she came in she took up one of the children's toys, and looking round the room, said, "Hanum, is this heaven?"

I told him we had come because we wished just

such homes as ours to spring up in every part of the land—homes where Christ is loved and trusted and obeyed, as their best Friend; but they could not have them, while the poor women were forbidden to read, and were treated as slaves, or, at best, as children.

"Yes, yes, hanum," he said, "education is a good thing."

"Have you a wife, brother?" I asked.

"Yes; but my father will not permit her to read. He has turned me out of doors because I will go to hear the Protestant preacher. He says that if I will go after the Protes, I may starve; he will not feed me; and I have come to the city for work."

He listened very earnestly when I told him that the Bible would bring all these blessings which we enjoy to their nation, and that he must not be disheartened, even if called to endure persecution for Christ's sake, for Christ himself has said, "In the world ye shall have tribulation: but be of good cheer; I have overcome the world."

The missionary experience of these few days was to me very pleasant. I would not have it blotted out from my life there for any consideration. We called it the "romance of missionary life," but there was much stern reality mingled with it; yet notwithstanding the hardships and fatigue, I enjoyed and learned much. At other times we went to more distant and larger places, and, did time and space allow, I would like to relate to my young readers the incidents of a month spent in Malatia, a longer time in Diarbekir, and, among others, of a visit to the *Kasabah*, or capital of the district of Geghi, five days' journey northeast from Harpoot. In some of these tours there was even more romance than in this, but that soon disappeared amid the hard, trying work to be done in all these places. But we always felt that the Master called us to go, and went with us; and we were safe and happy in his blessed companionship. Some turned a deaf ear to our message; others listened and were saved.

CHAPTER XIV.

DOES IT PAY?

THIS is just what Susie asked me as we concluded our last talk. "How could you leave your friends, and this pleasant home-land, mamma, to be a missionary? Does it pay?"

Others have asked the same question in the Old World and the New, and I would like to answer it here.

It does pay. Soul-saving is a noble work, so great that the Son of God said to his Father, "Send me; I will give my life for that lost world." He knew all the sorrows, the trials and temptations that awaited him in his foreign mission work, for such indeed it was. He left his home of glory, and came to this far-off world to save us. He humbled himself and became a little child, was born in a stable, lived with poor Joseph and Mary, and worked in the little shop at Nazareth with his reputed father, who was only a carpenter. It must have been trying for Jesus to spend thirty years thus, in preparation for his great work, but if we ask why it was so, we have but the one answer, "It was his Father's will;" and he "for the joy that was set before him endured the cross, despising the shame." And the missionary going forth to his work, with the love of Christ in his heart, can say the same. It would pay to leave all we hold dear and go to the ignorant and degraded, to bring up a people to a higher civilization, even if they are not Christianized; but the missionary has a sight of the souls that live for ever, and works not for time but for eternity.

When the young teacher from Franklin, Massachusetts, left her mother and sister to labor but a few years in Armenia, and then to die far away from the home of her youth, and be buried among strangers with not one of her kindred to follow her to that silent grave on the hillside, did it pay? True, loving, gentle hands were not wanting to minister to "our sunny May," as we called her, though mother and sister were not there. But when we saw the daughters of Armenia weeping around her lifeless form, telling of her youth, her sweetness, and her consecration to the Master whom she had taught them to love, we felt sure that it paid. Come to the place of prayer and hear these same loving friends: "Lord, bless the stricken mother far over the sea, who gave her loved daughter to labor for strangers whom she knew not, because she loved thee."

The missionary work is very trying. The missionary mother sending her children to the home land for education, may suffer more even than she who sends her dear ones to the foreign field. The latter go, at mature age, and, we might say, beyond the reach of harmful influences; the former, left at the tenderest age with strangers, often fail to receive the sympathy and watchful care they so much need when exposed to temptations, tried and perhaps sick. A mother was greatly comforted once, whose dear one was sick in America, by the simple, child-like prayers of these poor Armenian women. "Lord, bless the sick child in the far-off land, and make her well, because the mother stops here to labor for us." And the Lord hearkened and heard, and sent healing mercy, when the physicians had said, "There is no hope."

It is very hard for both parents and children to be thus separated, but I think our Heavenly Father gives such parents special grace to give up their children, and watches over the children we do believe with tenderest care. Such children usually become Christians at an early age. They have trials peculiar to themselves, but these are overruled for their good, and doubtless make them stronger men and women. I believe that if God calls us to do a special work, he will help us do that work. If, in doing it, we must be parted from our children, he will care for them, and will raise up friends to love and counsel them; and more, he will furnish the means to educate these children. Our loved ones may not have all they wish for, but they will have what is best for them.

I felt this very deeply, when, a few weeks since, I visited an asylum for inebriates, and was told that most of its inmates were the sons of wealthy parents. I thought the poor ministers and missionaries who are practising self-denial to keep their sons and daughters at school or college, were much better off even in this life; and our Saviour speaks of an eternal reward that awaits those who leave all for him. These missionaries and ministers might have been wealthy also if they had not chosen the life of self-denial for Christ; and then how would it have been with their children?

I would not imply that it is wrong to be rich; but I wish every rich man could feel as Pilibose, a stone-cutter in Harpoot, did, who came to one of the missionaries with a glowing face, saying, "Badvellie, I used to have great trouble in my business; but now I have made Jesus my partner, and I have no trouble." It would be well for all to have Jesus for a partner. He will help the poor in their self-denials, and the rich in their many temptations.

"There is another reason, mamma," says Susie, "why the missionary work must be very trying. Do you not remember the gentleman on the steamer asked you how an educated lady could live among such ignorant people?"

Yes, and he is not the only one who has asked that question; and yet that same gentleman would go to the gold mines with rude and wicked people, and sleep night after night in a hovel, for the sake of the shining dust he might bring home. He would leave wife and children and refined society, for the sake of worldly gain, or he would stand behind a counter day after day, and deal with the lowest and most degraded in our cities for money. We must have men to dig the gold, and men to stand behind the counter in all right kinds of business, and we must have missionaries; but if I must be judge, I should say the real self-denial is on the side of the first. The missionary's work is noble, soul-inspiring, and makes a nobleman of him in this life, and then he carries his treasures with him into eternity. He is scattering blessings broadcast in the world, which bring him in a harvest of joy, for Jesus says not a cup of cold water given in the name of a disciple shall lose its reward. And then if he is instrumental in saving one soul, that one may save another, and so the work goes on; and all these souls he will find at last in his Father's house in heaven. It is true that all our daily business, if done with an eye single to the glory of God, will be rewarded; but to lead souls to Christ will ever be our noblest work on earth, and will be crowned with the highest and best recompense.

It is moreover trying, to go to a strange land, and live among a people with a strange language, and strange habits and customs. We often feel "bound on four sides," as the Armenians say, but then is the time to look up. When difficulties thicken, and we are tempted to think we may have taken the wrong path, we pull out our "marching orders," and hear the Master say, "Go ye into all the world and preach the Gospel to every creature," and "Lo, I am with you alway, even unto the end of the world."

It is trying to be called "Satan," "the Evil One," "a leather face," "a leper," "a wolf in sheep's clothing;" but we read, "If they have called the master of the house Beelzebub, how much more shall they call them of his household?" It is hard to be stoned by a mob of women, to whom you are trying to give that gospel which alone can bring them up from their degraded condition. It is hard to have a crowd of women, yelling and shrieking, turn you out of doors at midnight, with nothing to shelter you from the pitiless November storm among the mountains. It is hard to have a woman drive you from her house, crying, "You shall never read that Bible here, not even on my doorstep. Begone, you dividers of families, you bringers of a new religion!" It is harder still to have those for whom you have faithfully labored tell you that you shall do no more for them, and perhaps accuse you of taking that which was given for them. But the hardest of all to the missionary is to have those who once bade fair to be earnest workers for Jesus, turn back, and, Judas-like, betray him.

But these dark clouds all have a silver lining. Yes, sometimes the lining is of a golden hue, it even sparkles like the diamond. Among these strange ones comes a poor woman who seizes your hands, and, with tears flowing fast down her withered cheeks, says, "Hanum, teach me how to pray." She has been to Jerusalem on a long pilgrimage. She will tell you that she has looked into the Savviour's sepulchre, and wept as Mary did; that she has stood on Calvary's mountain, and seen the cross upon which her Saviour died, and has taken her hard-earned money to the priest to have a ticket to heaven printed with indelible ink upon her arm. The image of Christ upon the cross has been pricked into her quivering flesh, to teach her that her Redeemer has suffered for her. What more could this heroic woman do? Is she not safe? She thought so. Her neighbors looked upon her as holy, as one to be honored. But the Bible has been read in her home, and old Haji Anna has heard, "Blessed are the pure in heart, for they shall see God." She had not found him who could purify the heart. The missionary has the golden privilege of leading her to the fountain where she may wash and be clean, and now she is casting her crown at His feet who redeemed her with his precious blood.

Come to the house of one of Christ's little ones and hear what she says, when a sorrow with a gloom darker than death overshadows her home, and rests most heavily upon her manly son, whose wife must be given up for attempted murder. "Let this not fall on Christ, and his little flock; let it fall on me and my father's house." Here is love to Christ's cause that shines above the love of the mother. Does it not pay to bring out of dead formalism a life such as this?

Did it not pay to teach little humpbacked Kolar, the *jewel* found on the side of old Taurus, who, when "bound on four sides," learned to looked up, up beyond the peaks of her native mountains, till she saw Him who alone could open the way for her?

Yes, sometimes there was even compound interest, as in the case of the women who mobbed the missionary. He afterwards found them with their "Gospel-hole" in the wall, trying to get from the chapel a few crumbs of the bread of life. Oh, how sweet it was to preach to them there! Perhaps you have never heard of this "Gospel-hole." When Susie's papa first went to the city of Choonkoosh, the women mobbed him. At a subsequent visit one of these same Amazonian women, got into a room next to the chapel, and made a little hole through the wall, in order to hear the missionary preach. And again, still later, when they heard that he was coming, and their new church was not quite ready for use, they got up a plastering bee, some mounting the ladder, trowel in hand, while others passed up the plaster, that when the missionary reached the place he might preach to them in the new house.

They were like the unpolished diamonds, needing only to be brought under the Master workman's hand to come out jewels of the first order.

Did it pay the missionary woman, who went to the little room on the housetop, and with stammering tongue taught the five or six little girls who came in there to learn to read? That little school has grown into the Female Department of Armenia College, where Miss West, Miss Fritcher, Mrs. Williams, and Miss Warfield, of sainted memory, have taught, and Misses Seymour and Bush are still teaching. Ask these grand women, whose superiors America cannot furnish, whether it pays to leave the land they love, and the friends dear as life, to labor among Armenia's daughters. Well might they point for answer to our Mount Holyoke in Eden, where there is almost a continuous revival, and very few leave the school without giving evidence that they belong to Christ, and expressing a desire to labor for their people.

They would point you to the nearly two hundred laborers who have gone out from this nursery of piety, to labor for their benighted sisters. Among these, is Amy, the once rude girl from a Koordish home. They would take you to the examination of her school, where the tall, dignified teacher goes through the exercises in a way that makes your very heart thrill with intense interest. Listen to her little girls as they recite their Bible lesson. Can the children in our American Sabbath-schools do better? Three short years ago that teacher was a poor wanderer among the Anti-Taurus mountains, without a ray of gospel light to cheer her wretched life.

They would tell you what Kohar, the humpback, is doing for Egin's proud sisters, who felt that no one could teach them. But she is the one God has chosen from a mean mountain village, to honor in this work. He brings one of Egin's "honorable women," clad in her silks, her hair white with the frost of seventy winters, to sit at Kohar's feet and learn to read God's word. No longer need the little cripple fear to go from house to house, for Nazloo Hanum is her pupil now, and none insult her. No longer does she write, "I am alone; I have no friends here, and I long for the dear teachers and friends in Harpoot;" but, "Praise the Lord with me, he has given me twelve sisters and many children, whom I cannot leave even to come back to my loved work of teaching in the Seminary. You can get another teacher, but who will care for the sisters and children here if I leave them?"

Then there are the Mariams and Martas, the Annas, the Saras and the Markareeds, doing in scores of villages, on plain and mountain-side, the blessed work of introducing Christian homes which we saw Eva doing in Aghansi, while schools taught by pupils of our Seminary are preparing hundreds of intelligent women to adorn and perpetuate these homes. Three years ago, in the 89 Protestant schools in the Harpoot mission field, there were, with 2,080 young men and boys under instruction, 965 girls; while 610 men and women were taught by "little teachers," who went from house to house to give lessons—a total of 3,655 persons under Bible instruction, leaving out of the estimate the large number taught in Armenian schools, which had been opened as a result of missionary influence.

Thus we see that thousands of the daughters of Armenia are waking up, and coming out of the bondage of ignorance, superstition, and degradation, to a new life of intelligent Christian civilization. Of the 1,200 members of churches, more than a third are women, and the proportion of female members is constantly increasing.

Come with me to the wilds of Koordistan, more than a week's journey from Harpoot, where, until recently, woman was too ignorant even to call on the saints, or the "mother of God,"and in her distress could only pray to the brazen bird on the Yezidee military standard, "O holy bird, hear us!" Here, patient, gentle Sara, the wife of Kavmé, the Koordish missionary, laid down her life after a few years' toil, but having labored long enough to convince some scores of the degraded sisters of these wilds what a Christian home may be. Kavmé was the first missionary sent out by the evangelical churches of Harpoot.

It was no small trial for Sara to leave her friends, and go among such a people, but I am sure that as she looks down now upon that interesting work in dark Koordistan, she feels that it has more than paid.

Or come with me to Husenik, Hooelie, Hulakegh, Percheng, Palu, Egin, and a score of other towns and cities, and see the crowds who gladly come to meet the missionary lady, crowds whose hostility, a few years ago, was only equalled by their ignorance. Notice the eagerness with which many of them listen to the story of the cross, hear the earnest prayers of some, and learn the story of their home-life, their struggle to rise, of the slow and painful but real progress they are making, and you will say, "Pay! why, it seems as if nowhere can work for Jesus be found which pays like this! I, too, must be a missionary!"

Many there are among these, it is true, who sadden our hearts by turning in scorn or indifference away from the gospel message. But multitudes do this on this side the ocean. We do not need to go to Armenia to find those to whom the gospel message is proving a savor of death unto death. For such let us labor more earnestly. And for such as we cannot reach by personal influence, let us labor by prayer, and by contributions, sanctified by prayer.

Yes, this work does pay; and every follower of Christ, whether old or young, rich or poor, should have some share in it. How can any who bear the name of Christ be indifferent to such a work—His work?

And we cannot but rejoice that many Christians are awake to this blessed work, and we have seen how, as one fruit of their prayers, and gifts, and labors, Armenia's daughters are coming up to take their places with us as workers for Christ. But, in our joy over these, let us not forget the millions of that land who are still sunk in little better than pagan ignorance, and among these their conquerors and rulers the proud followers of Mohammed. For them too a work is beginning in the Seminary, in a daily Turkish lesson, the aim of which is to prepare Armenia's daughters to tell the gospel story to their Moslem despisers and oppressors. May we not hope and believe that God has in store for these rescued Armenians the great privilege of carrying this gospel, which has elevated them, to the daughters of Islam who dwell in their country?

DOES IT PAY?

To darkness and to sin enslaved,
   In Satan's power I lay;
King Jesus broke my bonds—I'm saved;
   You ask me, "Does it pay?"

Rather ask Him, who suffered all,
   Gave all the gain to me,
Endured the scourge, the thorns, the cross,
   That I might rescued be.

He tells me he is satisfied;
   He loves to save from sin;
On earth his constant, only joy
   Was bringing sinners in.

And now he wears a glorious crown,
   Enthroned in power above,
He sends his promised Spirit down
   To do this work of love,

And says to me, "Go thou, and work,
   Lo I am with thee still."
. Though it paid not, I'd still work on,
   I love to do his will.

I would not leave it, if I might,
  For all the world could give;
I love to point poor souls to Him,
  And see them look and live.

And then He tells me, by-and-by
  He will in glory come,
To give his toiling children rest
  In his own heavenly home.

A starless crown I would not wear,
  Nor go to heaven alone;
My Saviour gives me work to do,
  I'll toil on till 't is done.

Sisters and children, will you help
  In such a work as this?
Then by-and-by we'll share its joy
  In heaven's unending bliss.

www.ingramcontent.com/pod-product-compliance
Lightning Source LLC
Chambersburg PA
CBHW022115160426
43197CB00009B/1030